Social work with lesbian, gay, bisexual and trans people

Making a difference

Julie Fish

BASW
BRITISH ASSOCIATION
OF SOCIAL WORKERS

First published in Great Britain in 2012 by

The Policy Press
University of Bristol
Fourth Floor
Beacon House
Queen's Road
Bristol BS8 1QU
UK

tel +44 (0)117 331 4054
fax +44 (0)117 331 4093
e-mail tpp-info@bristol.ac.uk
www.policypress.co.uk

North American office:
The Policy Press
c/o The University of Chicago Press
1427 East 60th Street
Chicago, IL 60637, USA
t: +1 773 702 7700
f: +1 773-702-9756
sales@press.uchicago.edu
www.press.uchicago.edu

British Library Cataloguing in Publication Data
A catalogue record for this book is available from the British Library.

Library of Congress Cataloging-in-Publication Data
A catalog record for this book has been requested.

ISBN 978 1 84742 803 5 paperback
ISBN 978 1 84742 804 2 hardcover

Cover design by The Policy Press.
Front cover: image kindly supplied by www.istock.com
Printed and bound in Great Britain by Hobbs, Southampton.
The Policy Press uses environmentally responsible print partners.

SOCIAL WORK IN PRACTICE series

Series editors: **Viviene Cree**, University of Edinburgh and
Steve Myers, University of Salford

"This series combines all the elements needed for a sound basis in 21st-century UK social work. Readers will gain a leading edge on the critical features of contemporary practice. It provides thoughtful and challenging reading for all, whether beginning students or experienced practitioners."
Jan Fook, Professor in Social Work Studies, University of Southampton

This important series sets new standards in introducing social workers to the ideas, values and knowledge base necessary for professional practice. These core texts are designed for students undertaking professional training at all levels as well as fulfilling the needs of qualified staff seeking to update their skills or move into new areas of practice.

Editorial advisory board:
Karen Bowler, The Policy Press
Suzy Braye, University of Sussex
Jim Campbell, Goldsmith's University of London
Gina Hardesty, Independent Consultant
Ravi Kohli, University of Bedfordshire
Jill Manthorpe, King's College London
Kate Morris, University of Birmingham
Joan Orme, University of Glasgow
Alison Shaw, The Policy Press
Charlotte Williams, Keele University

Other titles in the series:
Social work: Making a difference by Viviene Cree and Steve Myers
Social work and multi-agency working: Making a difference
edited by Kate Morris
Youth justice in practice: Making a difference by Bill Whyte
Radical social work in practice: Making a difference by Iain Ferguson
and Rona Woodward
Religion, belief and social work: Making a difference by Sheila Furness
and Philip Gilligan
Communicating with children and young people: Making a difference by
Michelle Lefevre

Contents

List of tables and figures

List of tables

List of figures

List of abbreviations

ADP   anti-discriminatory practice
BIHR   British Institute of Human Rights
CCETSW Central Council for Education and Training in Social Work
CQC   Care Quality Commission
CSCI   Commission for Social Care Inspection
DCA   Department for Constitutional Affairs
DCLG   Department for Communities and Local Government
DCSF   Department for Children, Schools and Families (from June 2007)
DfES   Department for Education and Skills
DH   Department of Health
EBL   enquiry-based learning
ECM   Every Child Matters
EHRC   Equality and Human Rights Commission
GSCC   General Social Care Council (the regulatory body for social work 2003–12)
HPC   Health Professions Council (the regulatory body for social work from 2012)
IASSW   International Association of Schools of Social Workers
IFSW   International Federation of Social Workers
ILGA   International Lesbian and Gay Association
LGB   lesbian, gay and bisexual
LGBT   lesbian, gay, bisexual and trans
NOS   National Occupational Standards
PCF   Professional Capabilities Framework (new curricula standards for social work)
PFC   Press For Change (trans rights organisation)
QAA   Quality Assurance Agency (sets curriculum standards in Higher Education)
SCIE   Social Care Institute for Excellence
SWRB   Social Work Reform Board
TOPSS   Training Organisation for the Personal Social Services
UKBA   UK Border Agency

Acknowledgements

I would like to thank colleagues and social work students at De Montfort University for their insights and experiences, in particular, Yateen Makwana, Sam Bennett and Maxine Magee. Thanks to Nettie for her patience and support while I was writing this book and to Steve for his sense of humour.

Introduction

Over the past decade, there have been profound social and legal changes for Lesbian, Gay, Bisexual and Trans (LGBT) people in the UK that impact on the practice of social work. These include the legal recognition of same-sex partnerships, eligibility to apply to adopt a child, protection from dismissal from employment, legal recognition of homophobic hate crime and rights of succession to a tenancy if a partner dies. Until the introduction of the Equality Act (Sexual Orientation) Regulations in 2007, there was no legislation to prohibit discrimination against LGBT people in public services. Changes in legislation have been accompanied by more positive social attitudes. In 1987, the British Social Attitudes Survey revealed that 75% of people believed that homosexuality was 'always or mostly wrong' (EHRC, 2009: 10). By 2008, the proportion of people holding such beliefs had fallen to 32%. 'Beyond tolerance', an online survey of 5,000 people for the Equality and Human Rights Commission (EHRC), showed that 84% would be happy or neutral to be treated by an openly LGBT doctor (EHRC, 2009). The survey also revealed that only a third of heterosexual men agreed that gay men could be 'equally good at bringing up children as other men' and they also agreed that lesbians and gay men will find it harder to adopt a child than other men and women (EHRC, 2009: 63). Beliefs that LGBT parents are second best have an impact on social work practice and may mean that LGBT people's parenting capacity is assessed less favourably than that of other people.

Hidden in social work services

Research by Barnardo's, the children's charity, highlighted that fewer than 4% of children (120 out of 3,200 children) were adopted by same-sex couples in England (Hill, 2011). This is a figure that was evenly split between couples who were and were not in a civil partnership. Information about LGBT people as users of social work is relatively uncommon. Although data are routinely collected on gender, 'race', disability and religion, public bodies have been reluctant to collect information about the sexual orientation of people using their services. This is partly because they do not see the case for monitoring sexual orientation and partly because of the perceived reluctance of LGBT people to disclose. *Beyond Tolerance: Making Sexual Orientation a*

Public Matter argued that understanding LGBT people's experiences of public services is a vital missing piece of the jigsaw:

> We live in a society where heterosexuality is the norm and other expressions of sexuality are hidden and this in turn has affected confidence in public expression of LGBT lifestyles. Assumptions perpetuate misunderstandings and people get treated differently as a result – sometimes unequally and unfairly.... There is a vital difference between privacy and invisibility. People have not been asked about sexual orientation until recently in official surveys and for public purposes, for example, service monitoring. As a result LGBT lifestyles have remained largely invisible. This lack of visibility and awareness has meant that significant disadvantage and discrimination has gone unnoticed and remained unchallenged. (EHRC, 2009: 12)

Without the acknowledgement that LGBT people may be users of services in residential care, mental health services or in services for people with learning disabilities, providers may not offer appropriate care. Social care providers have held a number of assumptions about LGBT people that mean they have not had a history of open engagement in service provision and these are critiqued below.

LGBT people are not a homogeneous group

It is estimated that 3.6 million LGBT people live in the UK and they are represented in every demographic group: they are old and young, black and minority ethnic people, women, disabled, and they may be working class and/or people of faith. They may also be asylum seekers or refugees, homeless people, prisoners, or people living in poverty. They are often assumed to be childless and to earn higher salaries than their heterosexual counterparts. Some of these assumptions imply that LGBT people are more privileged than other social groups. Social care providers located in smaller towns or in rural areas sometimes assume that there are no LGBT people living in the local community because of beliefs that they live only in large urban areas with an identifiable LGBT population. Stereotypes about what LGBT people look like give rise to the assumption that they can be easily identified by their appearance.

The right to a public life for LGBT people

Being LGBT is often seen as a private concern that is not relevant to the provision of care. Providers often do not know whether they have LGBT service users because they do not routinely monitor sexual orientation. Asking questions about sexual orientation is seen as intrusive and it elicits discomfort or embarrassment in professionals (Hinchliffe et al, 2005).

We don't want to offend other service users

A common response to discussion about the need to provide services for LGBT people is that other service users will feel uncomfortable. This may be a particular issue when people live in close proximity to each other. There has been a reluctance to offer same-sex older couples a shared room in a residential care home because of concerns about the reactions of other service users.

We are open to everyone anyway

In order to offer the same standard of service, social workers should take account of different needs and experiences. Treating everyone in the same way fails to acknowledge difference. It is the responsibility of the organisation to demonstrate that they are welcoming to LGBT people and ensure that services are appropriate.

There is no longer discrimination on the grounds of sexual orientation

Some providers argue that because legislation offers protection from discrimination, there are no longer distinct issues (eg a service provider may have offered support to an LGBT service user facing eviction from their home on the death of their partner because of the lack of tenancy rights). This assumption overlooks the fact that although there has been sex discrimination legislation for the past 40 years, it has not outlawed all instances of discrimination. Moreover, LGBT people have different family forms, networks and life experiences (adapted from Smith and Calvert, 2001: 8–12).

The lack of an evidence base

A major barrier to equitable social work practice is the lack of information about the specific needs of LGBT people. A recent report by the EHRC – *How Fair is Britain?* – highlighted the lack of large-scale quantitative data across a range of policy areas about LGBT people (EHRC, 2010); they are often described as a hidden population and are under-represented in research (Boehmer, 2002). Where possible, this book draws on research undertaken in the UK, but because of the dearth of UK-based research, studies conducted in the US (where a relatively large body of published work has been undertaken) are used to highlight relevant issues. There are, however, limits to the transferability of research findings from the US context to the UK as the cultural, legislative and social environment is very different. Some of this distinctiveness is evident in the organisation of welfare, the practice of social work and in the legal protections afforded to LGBT people (and these also differ between the different states of the US).

Sexual orientation or sexuality: what is meant by the terms?

This book uses the term sexual orientation rather than sexuality. Sexuality is a complex term that is commonly understood to refer to sexual activity, sensuality and sexual desire. In Foucault's (1978) classic theorisation, sexuality was confined to the domestic sphere and 'absorbed it into the serious function of reproduction' (Foucault, 1978: 1).

The use of the term sexuality in the context of social work practice is problematic because it is commonly used to refer to heterosexuality; moreover, in relation to LGBT people, it appears to emphasise the notion that they have sexualised identities (see later discussion). Although the term sexual orientation also has its limitations (eg it implies that sexual orientation is fixed rather than fluid), it is the preferred term in legislation and is in common use in central and local government policy documents.

Understanding sexual orientation

Alfred Kinsey et al (1953) first suggested that sexual orientation lay on a continuum of sexual behaviour. At the time, these views were groundbreaking because homosexuality had been considered to be a third sex. People were assumed to fit into discrete and exclusive categories where heterosexuality was considered normal and homosexuality was believed to be abnormal. Kinsey's research broke new ground because he suggested that homosexuality and heterosexuality lay on a continuum of expected sexual behaviour. Kinsey developed a seven-point rating scale for measuring sexual orientation from exclusively heterosexual to exclusively homosexual. Those who were exclusively heterosexual had no experience or desire for same-sex sexual activity, while those who were exclusively homosexual had no history of attraction or sexual activity with opposite-sex partners:

Kinsey Scale
0   Exclusively heterosexual
1   Largely heterosexual, but with incidental experience of same-sex behaviour
2   Largely heterosexual, but with distinct experience of same-sex behaviour
3   Equally heterosexual and homosexual
4   Largely homosexual, but with distinct experience of opposite-sex behaviour
5   Largely homosexual, but with incidental experience of opposite-sex behaviour
6   Exclusively homosexual. (Kinsey et al, 1953: 470)

Kinsey's scale emphasised sexual behaviour to the neglect of the meanings that people gave to their experiences. It is commonly assumed that being LGBT is a sexualised identity, that is, someone who is gay is defined by their sexual behaviour:

> Anne has been in a relationship with George for six years and after separating a year ago she has not had a sexual relationship with another man. Does this mean that because she is not having sex with a man, she is no longer heterosexual?

If the circumstances had been the same, but Anne had been in a relationship with Georgina, would Anne continue to be lesbian? There is also an assumption that if you have never had sex with someone of the same sex as yourself that you cannot be LGBT. If Anne was 14 years old and had never had sex with anyone, could she say that she is a bisexual young woman?

The diagram in Figure 1.1 is useful because it illustrates the interrelationship of sexual orientation and helps to understand the question: who is a lesbian, a gay man or a bisexual person? Is being LGBT determined by sexual behaviour, desire or political identification? Can someone be LGBT if they have never engaged in same-sex sexual behaviour? While heterosexuality is not defined by sexual activity, being lesbian, gay or bisexual commonly is so defined. Yet many LGBT people will be excluded by a definition that relies on sexual behaviour; young LGBT people may be attracted to someone of the same sex, but have not acted on that desire.

Figure 1.1: Dimensions of sexual orientation

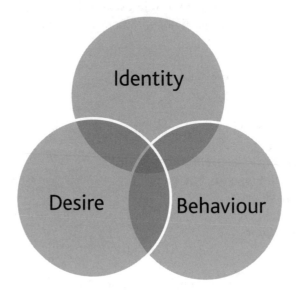

Source: Laumann et al (1994)

Desire

Some people are attracted to people of the same sex. They may spend time socialising with people of the same sex but may not act upon their attraction and may not describe themselves as LGBT.

Behaviour

Some people enjoy sexual relationships with people of the same sex but do not describe themselves as LGBT. Some people may be married or in long-term relationships with someone of the opposite sex.

Identity

Some people describe themselves as LGBT but do not have sexual relationships with people of the same sex, yet they may socialise with other LGBT people. Sometimes this is known as a politicised identity.

What causes sexual orientation?

People sometimes ask what causes homosexuality: theories about its origins range from nature (people are born this way) to nurture (family upbringing) (Fish, 2006). Theories of causation include the 'gay gene', biology or hormonal differences. Researchers have come up with some surprising claims that an increase in male hormones in the womb leads to differences in the length of lesbians' fingers (Williams et al, 2000), their cerebral functioning (Rahman et al, 2006) or inner ears (McFadden and Pasanen, 1998) leading to hearing loss in comparison to heterosexual women. Heteronormative assumptions give social privileges to heterosexuality by constructing it as natural and normal (see the glossary for a definition of the concept). The question 'What makes people heterosexual?' is not asked.

Coming out as LGBT service users

Social work is based on the concepts and assumptions of heterosexuality. Lesbians, gay men and bisexuals are presumed to be heterosexual; they are assumed to have the same needs as heterosexual people, or they are believed to be 'inferior' heterosexuals (see Fish, 2006: 9–10). Such values and attitudes influence LGBT decision-making when they access social work and social care. Questions that many LGBT people ask themselves before meeting service providers include: how relevant is knowledge about my sexual identity? Am I likely to feel more, or less, uncomfortable if my sexual orientation is known? How easy is it to 'pass' as heterosexual? Do I need advice that is tailored to meet my needs as an LGBT person? How accepting is the service provider likely to be? If the service provider exhibits heterosexist behaviour, are they also able to deny me (or make access difficult to) the care I need?

Black and minority ethnic LGBT people

The health and social care needs of LGBT people from black and minority ethnic (BME) communities is possibly the most under-researched field in queer studies. Yet, for a decade from the mid-1980s, there was a small but vibrant body of work that included early analysis of the intersection between racism and heterosexism in the writings of Audre Lorde (1984) and Valerie Mason-John (1995); discussion of homophobia by Hull et al (1982), Smith (1993) and Gomez and Smith (1994); alongside personal narratives of integrating multiple aspects of identity in Cole Wilson and Allen (1994) and Fashanu (1994). Classic, early studies conducted in the US investigated black lesbians' experiences of coming out to professionals (Cochran and Mays, 1988) and the impact of discrimination on the intimate relationships of black lesbians (Mays et al, 1993). The current absence has been taken as proof, in popular assumptions, that the numbers of BME LGBT people are comparatively small or even as an indication that homosexuality is a white problem or 'white disease' (Smith, 1993: 101). In a critique that challenged the unexamined assumptions of researchers, Beverly Greene (2003) proposed that studies have been conducted among people who are the most easily accessed in bars or clubs who are 'overwhelmingly white, middle class, young, able-bodied participants, most often urban, college student or well-educated populations' (Greene, 2003: 378).

BME LGBT people have fallen between the gaps in research disciplines. Research among LGBT people has neglected to consider LGBT people from BME communities – different sampling strategies may be required to recruit them to studies (Peplau et al, 1997). Studies conducted among BME populations have overlooked LGBT experiences by presuming the heterosexuality of participants and have never asked a question about sexual orientation (Greene, 2003).

There is, then, a dearth of research in any discipline and this absence is also reflected in the social work literature. In the US, however, researchers have begun to build a body of evidence and there has also been some consideration in social work journals of issues pertinent to conducting research among BME populations (Wheeler, 2003), of the religious needs of BME LGBT service users (Cutts and Park, 2009) and the needs of black lesbians who are users of social work services (Swigonski, 1995). The political, social and cultural context in North America may limit the transferability of the findings: social work practice in the US has roots in therapeutic practice. Some of the rights and freedoms that have been recently won in the UK and in Europe, such as Civil Partnership legislation, eligibility to adopt children, as well as employment benefits such as pensions, have been bitterly contested in the US.

LGBT people: a new alliance?

'Trans' describes a group of people who are gender variant in behaviour and preference, which includes people who are transgender, transsexual and people who cross-dress, and is the preferred term in the UK. New legal requirements mean that trans people have the same rights as everyone else to be protected from discrimination in their access to public services, including social work. The Gender Recognition Act 2004 enables trans people to apply for a new birth certificate and the Act also brings responsibilities for social workers in commissioning or providing services to meet needs. For example, trans people have the same rights as any other individual to adopt or foster a child; older trans people may have particular needs for personal care in residential care settings. The legislation brings duties for multidisciplinary care teams in relation to confidentiality. But while there is a substantial body of literature about the medical care of trans people, little is known about their needs for social care (Hines, 2007).

In the early 21st century, new alliances were formed that saw the inclusion of trans people's movements for equality across the public and voluntary sectors and in policy development, including in the Department of Health's Sexual Orientation and Gender Identity Advisory Group. There are, however, a number of key differences between trans people's concerns and those of lesbian, gay and bisexual people; for example, trans people's confidentiality is protected through legislation and the choice about public disclosure will be balanced alongside the decision to live their life in the acquired gender role. The distinctions between coming out as lesbian, gay or bisexual people and those of trans people are sometimes dichotomised: trans people are often represented as preferring to live their lives in stealth or passing but they may just as likely make the decision to come out. Discrimination on the grounds of gender identity is also distinctive and community networks and support may be less accessible due to the relative lack of infrastructure and history of engagement with trans communities. Mainstream research has predominantly focused on gender reassignment surgery to the exclusion of other concerns, while research conducted into trans people's health and social care needs have been subsumed within the larger LGBT research agenda. This often means that there is a lack of clarity about the key issues for trans people and the impression is created that a greater number of research studies have been conducted on trans people's health and social care needs than is the case: for this reason, trans people's needs are identified in a separate chapter. Throughout the book, the term LGBT is used to refer to issues that are common across the spectrum of sexual orientation and gender identity and in recognition of joint organising and shared concerns.

The aims, approach and structure for this book

This book is about how student social workers can make a difference in the lives of LGBT people. It aims to provide an introductory text for students and social work educators on qualifying programmes to provide a focus for debate and stimulate further learning. The book specifically engages with the concerns and experiences that are distinctive for LGBT people in their access to and use of social work services. By drawing on an existing body of evidence, the book aims to offer a framework to underpin knowledge, skills and values to develop best practice in social work with LGBT people.

Enquiry-Based Learning

Enquiry-Based Learning (EBL) describes an approach to learning that is underpinned by a process of enquiry (Cree and Myers, 2008). Typically, students work together in small groups on scenarios from social work practice that are sufficiently open-ended to allow for more than one course of action. Working within an identified task, students take responsibility for their own learning and pursue their own lines of enquiry. The approach takes as its starting point that people learn through experience and build upon previous learning, which may be derived from feeling, thinking, watching and doing (Kolb, 1984). Students are more likely to assimilate learning where they have discussed it with others, incorporated it in their practice or shared their skills with others. A framework for supporting EBL includes:

- Understand the scenario.
- Identify resources.
- Analyse the information (and apply relevant social work theories or methods).
- Identify alternative courses of action.
- Present the findings.

EBL will be used in this book as an approach to learning where students work in small groups on a case study derived from social work practice. Their task is to use the practice scenario to develop their understanding: identifying learning objectives and resources, and making decisions about an appropriate course of action. The scenario is introduced at the beginning of each chapter and the subsequent discussion illustrates some of the themes in the 'case study'.

Solution-focused approaches

Solution-focused practice is an approach that fits well with EBL and may be particularly relevant for social work in mental health or substance misuse. The approach is useful for working with service users to make changes to their current life circumstances and is distinctive because one of its core principles is that intervention does not have to be long-term and that change can happen quickly (O'Connell, 2007). There has often been an assumption in therapeutic approaches that for change to have any lasting value, it must be lengthy and deep. In contrast to other approaches that focus on problems, in solution-focused work the practitioner works with the service user to identify solutions together. It takes a no-blaming approach and focuses on behaviour rather than emotions. The problem is the problem, not the service user, and it seeks to build on aspects of his or her life that are problem-free (Myers, 2008). This approach is useful in work with LGBT service users because it avoids pathology and the identification of deficits. Solution-focused approaches are action-oriented towards the future and are based on practical assumptions:

- Problems are part of life – overcoming them is what makes us human.
- Problems are embedded in language – change may involve unpicking the assumptions around the problem.
- Problems take place in the interaction between the person and the social environment – problems are not inside someone.
- Understanding a problem does not have to precede solving it – the understanding can emerge later, if at all.
- People are resilient problem-solvers.
- People often do not remember or learn from times when they use 'solutions'.
- People engage more with an approach that builds on their strengths than one which highlights their deficiencies.
- People are more likely to implement customised strategies than formulaic 'one-size-fits-all' solutions.
- It is more effective to build on what works than to get someone to do something for the first time.
- Small steps tend to be more helpful than big ones (see O'Connell, 2007: 24).

Social workers form a collaborative relationship with the service user, create a climate for change, clarify as far as possible the service user's goals, highlight the service user's resources and negotiate tasks (see O'Connell, 2007: 37).

Key features

Each chapter outlines a practice scenario to inform critical reflection on some of the issues identified in the chapter and provides references to research relevant to the chapter theme.

Structure

Chapter 2 outlines the context for considering sexual orientation and gender identity in social work including the General Social Care Council (GSCC) *Codes of Practice* and the key principles of the Professional Capabilities Framework (PCF) for social work students and newly qualified social workers. The regulatory functions of the GSCC for qualifying social work education will transfer to the College of Social Work in 2012. The chapter considers the implications of relevant articles of the Human Rights Act 1998 for LGBT people and provides an overview of the UK legislative context.

Chapter 3 introduces three theoretical perspectives of relevance to sexual orientation and gender identity: cultural competence, anti-discriminatory practice and human rights approaches. The chapter presents a critique of each approach and provides a practical activity to support student learning.

Chapter 4 brings together the skills, knowledge and values needed to develop inclusive practice with trans people. Trans people have been largely overlooked in social work research and practice and the chapter considers relevant concepts and underpinning knowledge including gender identity and nonconformity, experiences of discrimination, and relevant policy and legislation. Key issues relevant for social work include mental health, domestic abuse, homelessness and residential care, and older trans people.

Chapter 5 considers how child care policy, such as Every Child Matters, can be used to understand some of the issues facing LGBT children and young people. It considers relevant policy, legislation and underpinning knowledge. Key domains of the assessment framework are used to identify the potential developmental needs of LGBT young people.

Chapter 6 explores social work practice with older LGBT people including perceptions of ageing, personalisation, residential care and end-of-life care. It considers the implications of different family structures and personal networks for social work. It identifies existing good practice in work with older LGBT people.

Chapter 7 considers the mental health of LGBT people within the historical context of stigma and marginalisation. The impact of discrimination on LGBT people's mental health and their use of mental health services are discussed. The mental health of young people, people from BME communities and older people is also discussed.

Chapter 8 considers the needs and experiences of LGBT people with physical or learning disabilities. It discusses the social and medical model of disability and explores relevant policy and legislation. In particular, it considers identity development and coming out, personal and sexual relationships, and disability hate crimes. Good practice in assessments and care planning are identified.

Chapter 9 explores the reasons why social workers need to be aware of substance use in LGBT communities. It identifies relevant practice models in social work with substance misusers, in particular, motivational interviewing. It examines key data from the British Crime Survey about prevalence and patterns of substance misuse in LGBT communities.

Chapter 10 examines the global context for social work and LGBT people. It explores the consequences of unequal protections worldwide for LGBT people that force many to flee their countries of origin and to seek asylum. Although being LGBT is recognised as a protected status in international asylum legislation, the majority of LGBT asylum seekers experience considerable difficulties in making their claim in the UK. This chapter identifies the distinctive issues for LGBT asylum seekers. The chapter also identifies a small body of work that considers trans people's experiences of asylum.

The requirement to consider sexual orientation in social work

Social work is practised with those who are among the disadvantaged in society; its core aim is to work collaboratively with people to bring about change in their lives. In order to work alongside people to enable them to bring about lasting change, social workers must have attitudes and values that demonstrate their recognition of people's lives and circumstances.

The international requirement for social workers to promote social justice for lesbian, gay and bisexual people is included alongside those of other equality grounds in the code of ethics developed jointly by the International Federation of Social Workers (IFSW) and the International Association of Schools of Social Work (IASSW) in 2004. It requires social workers to promote social justice not only in relation to the people with whom they work but also in society generally:

> Social workers have a responsibility to challenge negative discrimination on the basis of characteristics such as ability, age, culture, gender or sex, marital status, socio-economic status, political opinions, skin colour, racial or other physical characteristics, sexual orientation, or spiritual beliefs. (IFSW and IASSW, 2004: s 4.2)

With the development of the degree in social work in the UK, a number of organisations have been responsible for setting standards for best practice in social work. The General Social Care Council (GSCC) is currently the awarding authority for the degree and the profession's regulatory body in England and Wales until these functions transfer to the College of Social Work and the Health Professions Council in 2012. The GSCC *Codes of Practice* (2010) (agreed across the four countries of the UK) describe the standards of professional conduct required of social care workers and student social workers in their everyday work: 'treating each person as an individual', 'respecting diversity and different cultures and values', 'promoting equal opportunities' and 'protecting the rights and promoting the interests of service users and carers' (GSCC, 2010: 5–6).

The Social Work Reform Board, which was set up following the death of Baby Peter, proposed a new Professional Capabilities Framework that identified nine key principles underpinning qualifying social work programmes and the status of Newly Qualified Social Worker. These are:

- *Professionalism* – Identify and behave as a professional social worker, committed to professional development.
- *Values and Ethics* – Apply social work ethical principles and values to guide professional practice.
- *Diversity* – Recognise diversity and apply anti-discriminatory and anti-oppressive principles in practice.
- *Rights, Justice and Economic Well-being* – Advance human rights and promote social justice and economic well-being.
- *Knowledge* – Apply knowledge of social sciences, law and social work practice theory.
- *Critical Reflection and Analysis* – Apply critical reflection and analysis to inform and provide a rationale for professional decision-making.
- *Intervention and Skills* – Use judgement and authority to intervene with individuals, families and communities to promote independence, provide support and prevent harm, neglect and abuse.
- *Contexts and Organisations* – Engage with, inform and adapt to changing contexts that shape practice. Operate effectively within own organisational frameworks and contribute to the development of services and organisations. Operate effectively within multi-agency and inter-professional settings.
- *Professional Leadership* – Take responsibility for the professional learning and development of others through supervision, mentoring, assessing, research, teaching, leadership and management (see Social Work Reform Board, 2010).

The Quality Assurance Agency (QAA) is responsible for maintaining academic standards for all programmes in higher education; the subject benchmark statements define the academic discipline in terms of its coherence and identity and outline the range of skills, understanding and knowledge required for practice. Social workers should understand the relationships of 'social differences (for example, social class, gender, ethnicity, age, sexuality and religious belief) to the problems of inequality and differential need faced by service users' (QAA, 2008: 8).

The degree combines academic learning alongside practice learning and students are currently required to undertake placements in social work and social care agencies to develop their skills and competencies. The National Occupational Standards (NOS) define the skills, values and knowledge that student social workers must demonstrate and these identify 21 units of competence (TOPSS, 2002). Sexuality is identified in the performance criteria of only two of the elements (by comparison, religion is identified in only one), which require students to 'Identify the nature of the relationship and the processes required to develop purposeful relationships, taking account of ethnicity, gender, age, disability, sectarianism and sexuality issues' (TOPSS, 2002: 27).

The commitment to take action to counter discrimination, inequality and injustice was identified as integral to the profession of social work. These values were explicit in the Code of Ethics developed by the British Association of Social Workers (BASW), which includes a clear commitment to anti-discriminatory practice: social workers should:

> Ensure that they do not act out of prejudice against any person or group, on any grounds, including origin, ethnicity, class, status, sex, sexual orientation, age, disability, beliefs or contribution to society. (BASW, 2002: s 3.2.2)

In a comparative analysis, the inclusion of sexual orientation in professional codes of practice, academic training standards and codes of ethics was reviewed across three countries: the US, Canada and the UK. The US had the clearest mandate for the inclusion of sexual orientation in social work, while the picture in the UK was ambiguous (Mulé, 2006). It might be argued, however, that over the past decade, a more supportive legislative framework has emerged in which there is legal sanction for LGBT rights.

International legislation: human rights and LGBT people

The Human Rights Act 1998 formally came into force in October 2000. It incorporated the European Convention on Human Rights into UK law, thereby allowing individuals to petition the domestic courts in defence of their Convention rights, rather than having to take their claim to the European Court of Human Rights in Strasbourg. The Act brought into law a number of rights and freedoms that were first described in the Universal Declaration of Human Rights in 1948. The events of the Second World War had shown the international community what can happen when some people are treated as less human than others.

Over the past decade, human rights have increasingly shaped approaches to social justice and have become embedded in the delivery of services. They form part of what it means to be human and they set out basic needs. They provide a framework to protect everyone's rights and play a key role in tackling inequality. They give rise to five core principles – fairness, respect, equality, dignity and autonomy, often known by the acronym FREDA – which should inform the way that users of services are treated. The Human

Rights Act 1998 marks an important departure from existing equality and diversity legislation, which has sometimes been seen as reactive (enabling redress in the courts by challenging discrimination once it has occurred). Existing equality legislation has prohibited discrimination and consequently has sometimes been seen to have a negative orientation (avoiding getting it wrong) rather than a positive orientation (improving people's lives).

The Human Rights Act 1998 sets out 16 rights and freedoms that enable the fulfilment of our basic needs. The UK Human Rights Act makes part of UK law the following rights from the European Convention (note that Article 1 identifies overarching rights and freedoms):

- The right to life (Article 2).
- The right not to be tortured or treated in an inhuman or degrading way (Article 3).
- The right to be free from slavery or forced labour (Article 4).
- The right to liberty (Article 5).
- The right to a fair trial (Article 6).
- The right to no punishment without law (Article 7).
- The right to respect for private and family life, home and correspondence (Article 8).
- The right to freedom of thought, conscience and religion (Article 9).
- The right to freedom of expression (Article 10).
- The right to freedom of assembly and association (Article 11).
- The right to marry and found a family (Article 12).
- The right not to be discriminated against in relation to any of the rights contained in the European Convention (Article 14).
- The right to peaceful enjoyment of possessions (Article 1 of Protocol 1).
- The right to education (Article 2 of Protocol 1).
- The right to free elections (Article 3 of Protocol 1).
- Abolition of the death penalty (see BIHR, 2007a: 20).

Human rights have often been seen in the context of an infringement of them in other countries or in times of conflict, but this is a limited understanding of their possibilities for making a positive difference. Providers of health and social care cannot begin to improve people's health and well-being unless they ensure that human rights are respected. Articles 7–10 are qualified rights; this means that the state can restrict the right if it is in the person's best interests, on grounds of public safety or if it is proportionate and for a legitimate aim. Five human rights are particularly relevant to health and social care; these are first outlined in the following and then their implications are discussed in relation to the new rights and freedoms for LGBT people.

Article 3: the right not to be tortured or treated in an inhuman or degrading way

Degrading treatment refers to treatment that is 'humiliating and undignified' and can include washing or dressing service users without regard to dignity (BIHR, 2007b: 37). Article 3 offers protection for trans service users in receipt of personal care. In domiciliary or residential care, a trans person may need help with washing and dressing; they have the right to be treated with respect and dignity. They may need help to protect their sense of identity and self-esteem, for example, by the daily removal of facial hair (Hartley and Whittle, 2003).

Article 8: the right to respect for private and family life

The concept of a private life means that an individual has the right to live their own life taking into account the rights and freedoms of others. The right to a private life is relevant in social work and social care because any intervention in the way a person lives their life may affect their right to respect for private and family life. LGBT issues are used as examples in the Department for Constitutional Affairs (DCA) guidance document for public authorities (DCA, 2006: 26):

- freedom to choose one's own sexual identity;
- freedom to choose how one looks and dresses.

Private life includes 'personal choices, relationships, physical and mental well being, access to personal information and participation in community life' (BIHR, 2007a: 39). This is a wide-ranging right; examples of what it might include in health and social care are:

- privacy on hospital wards and in care homes;
- family visits;
- sexual and other relationships;
- participation in social and recreational activities;
- personal records including health and social work;
- independent living;
- closure of residential care homes or hospitals;
- separation of families due to residential care placements (see BIHR, 2007a: 39).

Family has been an important concept for LGBT people. The Local Government Act 1988 described LGBT people as having only 'pretended family relationships'. It has had wide-ranging implications for the recognition of LGBT families in social work because they were not eligible to apply to adopt a child, they were seen as unfit parents and were often denied custody of their biological children, and when a person in an intimate relationship had died, the surviving partner was denied their tenancy and forced to leave their family home. In the Human Rights Act 1998, family life is interpreted broadly and it extends beyond blood relatives. This has implications for LGBT families as they are likely to have broader ideas of family, which include friends, ex-partners and extended social networks, and this is described by the notion of 'families of choice'. This has enabled trans people to maintain the privacy of their gender transition and it has underpinned the rights of LGBT people in respect of notions of families of choice.

The right to a private life can also include the right to have personal information about the disclosure of LGBT identity in a core assessment, care plan or other social work record kept private and confidential. Any disclosure of personal information about someone to another person or body is likely to affect a person's right to their private life under Article 8. When making decisions about human rights (in this case record-keeping and information sharing), account should be taken of a person's rights regarding their need for protection from harm, abuse or neglect and they need to be balanced against those of other members of the family and of the broader community (DCA, 2006).

This right may be relevant for social work in relation to:

■ confidentiality about trans people's gender identity status; and
■ recognition of the different structures and need of LGBT families.

Article 12: the right to marry and found a family

This article enabled the introduction of the Civil Partnership Act 2004, which gave same-sex couples the equivalent rights to those conferred by marriage. In the case of *Goodwin v UK*, the European Court interpreted this article as providing post-operative trans people with the right to marry. The Gender Recognition Act 2004 allows trans people, who have obtained legal recognition for their gender (whether or not they are post-operative), to marry a person of the opposite gender.

This right may be relevant for social work in relation to:

■ an older same-sex couple in a civil partnership having their relationship considered when making decisions if they have different needs for residential care.

Article 14: the right not to be discriminated against

Article 14 only protects people in exercising their rights contained in the European Convention. It does not give people a general right to protection. Sexual orientation is included within the term 'other status'. Discrimination takes place when someone is treated in a different way as compared to someone else in the same situation. The human rights definition of discrimination allows circumstances when it will reduce inequality to treat people differently ('positive discrimination', an example of which has been the use of all-women shortlists for selection as a political candidate). Such treatment would be in breach of Article 14 if a legitimate aim could not be demonstrated. However, it is worth noting that if people with 'different needs are treated in the same way, this would be discriminatory' (BIHR, 2007b: 40).

Article 14 has been successfully invoked under the Human Rights Act on behalf of a gay couple who wished to be treated in the same way as a heterosexual couple for the purposes of one partner succeeding the other under a tenancy (Fish, 2006).

Article 2 of Protocol 1: the right to education

This is not an absolute right, but it means that a person has a right not to be denied access to the existing educational system. This is an important right for young LGBT people because homophobic bullying and harassment have significant consequences affecting educational attendance, attainment and well-being. Incidents of bullying can lead to dropping out from school and low self-esteem. Verbal expressions of homophobia and transphobia are commonplace and the word 'gay' is commonly used in a derogatory way (FRA, 2009).

This right may be relevant for social work in relation to:

- a looked-after child experiencing homophobic bullying;
- education social workers working with a truanting child.

Practice scenario

A residential home for people with learning disabilities provided support for service users who wanted to participate in social activities. A gay man with learning disabilities who was socially isolated asked his support worker if he could accompany him to a gay pub. His request was refused even though heterosexual service users were regularly supported to attend pubs of their choice.

Question

Identify the relevant articles of the Human Rights Act 1998 that would support his request.

You may wish to consider mental capacity, a balanced approach to sexual health information and strategies for keeping safe. He should have access to appropriate information in the same way as a heterosexual young man with learning disabilities.

The UK legislative context for LGBT people

The path to equal rights for LGBT people has been long and arduous. Legislation that would normally afford protection conferred inferior rights for LGBT people (Fish, 2007). Throughout the 1990s, change in the legal framework was piecemeal and often vigorously opposed (Waites, 2003); in some cases, the Parliament Act was used to enforce change because of the weight of opposition to LGBT equality. The requirement to consider sexual orientation in public services, including social work, was first introduced by the Equality Act (Sexual Orientation) Regulations 2007. This legislation prohibited discrimination in access to goods, services and facilities for lesbian, gay and bisexual people and means that they can expect the same standard of treatment as the rest of the population. Sexual orientation was only recently recognised as an equality ground: protection from discrimination had been afforded on the grounds of gender since 1975, 'race' since 1976, disability since 1995 and religion since 2006. Protection for older people and for trans people was only introduced in 2008. Equality legislation in the UK was complex and many argued that a hierarchy of inequalities had been created where some equality strands were more equal than others (Fish, 2006). For example, public-sector duties required public bodies to take account of gender, 'race' and disability in the commissioning and delivery of services. The Equality Act 2010 was introduced to streamline existing legislation and to offer the same level of protection to each of the six equality strands (now termed protected characteristics) – age, disability, gender, race, religion and belief, and sexual orientation and gender identity – and it recognised three additional characteristics – marriage and civil partnership, pregnancy, and maternity – and introduced a public-sector duty to reduce inequalities arising from socio-economic disadvantage. Provisions of relevance include:

■ applying the European definition of indirect discrimination to all protected characteristics;
■ creating a basic framework of protection against direct and indirect discrimination, harassment, and victimisation in services and public functions, premises, work, education, associations, and transport; and
■ levelling up protection for people experiencing discrimination because of who they are perceived to be, or because they are associated with someone who has a protected characteristic.

The Act simplified 116 pieces of equality legislation and prevents discrimination, harassment and victimisation, promotes good relations between groups, and offers protection for both direct (section 13) and indirect (section 19) discrimination. The newly elected Coalition government made an explicit commitment to equality on the grounds of sexuality in its *Programme for Government*:

> The Government believes that there are many barriers to social mobility and equal opportunities in Britain today, with too many children held back because of their social background, and too many people of all ages held back because of their gender, race, religion or sexuality. We need concerted government action to tear down these barriers and help to build a fairer society. (HMG, 2010c: 18)

Key questions

➲ How can social workers work towards inclusive practice with LGBT people?
➲ What knowledge, skills and attitudes should social workers demonstrate in their practice?

Exercise 1: Reflecting on own values

- What were the values you were brought up with relating to LGBT people?
- What were the attitudes of your friends and school mates?
- How do you think your values might affect the way you work with LGBT service users?
- Do you know LGBT people in your personal life?

Exercise 2: Social work values and LGBT people

GSCC *Code of Practice*:

- Treating each person as an individual.
- Respecting confidential information and clearly explaining agency policies about confidentiality to service users and carers.
- Promoting the independence of service users and assisting them to understand and exercise their rights.

In relation to each of the codes:

- Discuss how good communication with LGBT people should reflect the values contained in the code.
- Why is confidentiality important for LGBT service users?
- How can you promote independence among LGBT service users?
- Think about and discuss what the code means and why following it is vital to good social work practice with LGBT people.

Overview of UK legislation

1885 The Criminal Law Amendment Act (the Labouchere Amendment)
This created the offence of gross indecency and made all sexual acts between men illegal. It became known as the 'blackmailer's charter'.

1967 Sexual Offences Act
Decriminalised homosexuality between two consenting men, in private, providing both were over 21.

1988 Local Government Act

Under section 28:

A local authority shall not:

(a) intentionally promote homosexuality or publish material with the intention of promoting homosexuality;
(b) promote the teaching in any maintained school of the acceptability of homosexuality as a pretended family relationship.

Nothing above shall be taken to prohibit the doing of anything for the purpose of treating or preventing the spread of disease.

1990 Human Fertilisation and Embryology Act

Artificial insemination was only to be provided if the need of the child for a father was considered; in practice it was often used to exclude lesbians.

1994 Criminal Justice Act

The Act lowered the age of consent for gay men from 21 to 18, but did not remove other restrictions from the 1967 Act. A new offence of abuse of trust was introduced. Sexual relationships, whether heterosexual or homosexual, between young people aged 16–18 and adults in a position of authority, like teachers, were made unlawful. Same-sex sexual behaviour in the armed forces was no longer treated as a criminal offence.

1997 Sexual Offenders Act

This Act required courts to place convicted sex offenders on a register. Men convicted of offences (including the younger person) before the lowering of the age of consent did not have their convictions quashed.

1998 Human Rights Act

The Human Rights Act 1998 makes it unlawful for public services to act in a way that infringes an individual's rights and freedoms under the European Convention on Human Rights.

1999 Sex Discrimination (Gender Reassignment) Regulations

These regulations made it illegal to discriminate against someone who 'intends to undergo, is undergoing or has undergone gender reassignment'.

2000 ACPO Guidelines for hate crimes

The Association of Chief Police Officers (ACPO) produced a manual for the police service's approach to identifying and combating hate crime towards LGBT people.

2000 Sexual Offences Act
The age of consent for gay men was lowered to 16: this is now the same as for heterosexuals. Because of fierce opposition in the House of Lords, this legislation was passed by use of the Parliament Act in January 2001.

2001 Criminal Injuries Compensation Scheme
The scheme was revised by the Home Office to include long-term same-sex partners as qualifying relatives in fatal accidents.

2002 Adoption and Children Act
Although there has never been a law preventing LGBT individuals from adopting children, there were a number of government circulars which suggested that LGBT people were not suitable as parents. In practice, LGBT people could adopt as single people, but could not apply to jointly adopt. The Act was subsequently amended by the Civil Partnership Act 2004, which introduced provisions to enable same-sex couples to apply to jointly adopt children.

2002 Housing law (*Ghaidan v Mendoza*)
This Law Lords' judgment gave the right to same-sex couples to succeed to a tenancy in the event of the death of a partner. It stated that a person who had lived in a permanent homosexual relationship with the original tenant of rented accommodation could succeed, on the partner's death, to the tenancy and become a protected statutory tenant as the 'surviving spouse of the late partner'.

2003 Sexual Offences Act
The offences of gross indecency and buggery, which particularly targeted gay men, have been deleted from the statutes. There is a concern regarding a new offence of 'sexual activity in a public lavatory'. The Act criminalises sexual behaviour that a person knew, or ought to have known, was likely to cause distress, alarm or offence to others in a public place. Some gay men are worried that this offence will allow the police to continue to stigmatise them.

2003 Criminal Justice Act
This legislation does not create an offence for homophobic assault. However, it ensures that where an assault involved or was motivated by hostility or prejudice based on sexual orientation (actual or perceived), the judge is required to treat this as an aggravating factor. Section 146 of the Act was implemented in 2005 allowing courts to impose tougher sentences.

2003 Local Government Act
This legislation repealed the provisions of the 1988 Local Government Act (including section 28).

2003 Employment Equality (Sexual Orientation) Regulations
These regulations prevent employers refusing to employ people because of their sexual identity and also protect workers from direct abuse and homophobia from colleagues. Employers have to ensure that benefits given to opposite-sex partners can also be claimed by same-sex partners (unless the benefit is offered only to married couples).

2004 Gender Recognition Act
This legislation allows a person of either gender to apply for a Gender Recognition Certificate. An application is made to the Gender Recognition Panel and must meet the following conditions: the person has or has had gender dysphoria; they have lived in the acquired gender in the two years up to the date when the application is made; and they intend to live in their acquired gender for the rest of their life. The Act allows for the full legal recognition of the acquired gender for trans people.

2004 Domestic Violence, Crime and Victims Act
The Act recognises for the first time that same-sex couples experience domestic abuse. The Safety and Justice White Paper proposed the main provisions on domestic violence under the three key headings of prevention, protection, and justice and support.

2004 Civil Partnership Act
The Act provides same-sex couples who form a civil partnership with parity of treatment in a wide range of legal matters with those opposite-sex couples who enter into a civil marriage. Provisions in the Act include:

* a duty to provide reasonable maintenance for the civil partner and any children of the family;
* civil partners to be assessed in the same way as spouses for child support;
* equitable treatment for the purposes of life assurance;
* employment and pension benefits;
* recognition under intestacy rules;
* access to fatal accidents compensation;
* protection from domestic violence; and
* recognition for immigration and nationality purposes.

The legislation was implemented on 5 December 2005 and (with the 15-day waiting period) the first civil partnerships were registered on 21 December 2005.

2006 Equality Act

This legislation outlawed discrimination on the grounds of religion and belief. Protection from discrimination on the grounds of sexual orientation was subsequently introduced by the following regulations.

2007 Equality Act (Sexual Orientation) Regulations

This legislation makes it unlawful for a person providing goods, facilities or services to members of the public to discriminate against anyone on the grounds of sexual orientation. This legislation protects heterosexual people as well as LGBT people. Except for some very precise exemptions, it is irrelevant whether the goods, facilities or services are offered for money or not, and they apply to all sectors and to organisations carrying out a function on behalf of a public authority.

2008 Human Fertilisation and Embryology Act

The Act recognises same-sex couples as legal parents of children conceived through the use of donated sperm, eggs or embryos. These provisions enable, for example, the civil partner of a woman who carries a child via in vitro fertilisation (IVF) to be recognised as the child's legal parent.

The Act retains a duty to take account of the welfare of the child in providing fertility treatment, but replaces the reference to 'the need for a father' with 'the need for supportive parenting' – hence valuing the role of all parents.

2010 Equality Act

This Act recognised sexual orientation and gender identity as protected characteristics and extends protection to include discrimination, harassment and victimisation. It harmonised existing equality and anti-discrimination legislation conferring equal protections across the nine protected characteristics, introducing a public-sector equality duty for sexual orientation and gender identity, and requiring public bodies to foster good relations. It further required public bodies to advance equal opportunities by:

- removing or minimising disadvantages suffered by persons who share a relevant protected characteristic;
- taking steps to meet the needs of persons who share a relevant protected characteristic that are different from the needs of persons who do not share it; and

> • encouraging persons who share a relevant protected characteristic to participate in public life or in any other activity in which participation by such persons is disproportionately low.

Further reading

BASW (British Association of Social Workers) (2002) *Code of Ethics for Social Workers*, Birmingham: BASW.

BIHR (British Institute of Human Rights) (2007a) *Human Rights in Health Care: A Framework for Local Action*, London: Department of Health.

BIHR (2007b) 'Human Rights Act: changing lives'. Available at: http://www.bihr.org.uk/sites/default/files/BIHR%20Changing%20Lives%20FINAL_0.pdf

FRA (European Union Agency for Fundamental Rights) (2009) 'Homophobia and Discrimination on Grounds of Sexual Orientation and Gender Identity in the EU Member States'. Available at: http://www.fra.europa.eu/fraWebsite/research/publications/publications_per_year/pub-LGBT-2010-update_en.htm (accessed 27 February 2011).

IFSW (International Federation of Social Workers) and IASSW (International Association of Schools of Social Work) (2004) *Ethics in Social Work: Statement of Principles*, Berne, Switzerland: IFSW.

QAA (Quality Assurance Agency) (2008) *Subject Benchmark Statement for Social Work*, Gloucester: The Quality Assurance Agency for Higher Education.

TOPSS (Training Organisation for Personal Social Services) (2002) *National Occupational Standards for Social Work.*, Leeds: Skills for Care.

Waites, M. (2003) 'Equality at Last? Homosexuality, Heterosexuality and the Age of Consent in the United Kingdom', *Sociology*, 37(4), 637–55.

3 Theoretical perspectives in social work with LGBT people

Introduction

Linking theory and practice is something that many practitioners and social work students grapple with. Theory is sometimes perceived as separate from practice and an aspect of social work learning that takes place predominantly in the university. The complexities of people's lives do not appear to fit into a neat box labelled theory. But theory provides a rationale for social work interventions (why one course of action is more appropriate than another), can aid understanding of the processes and the barriers that people may experience in their everyday lives, and can help to clarify potential outcomes. Theory helps social workers to guard against 'quick-fix' solutions and helps move the beginning practitioner from unconscious incompetence to conscious competence (Luft and Ingham, 1955).

In comparison to other social divisions, there has been relatively little theoretical development in social work and sexual orientation (for exceptions, see Hicks, 2005). Over a decade ago, Hardman (1997) critiqued the lack of social work models available to inform the development of good practice in work with service users. When social workers were asked to discuss their responses to practice scenarios, many of them had not considered the sexual orientation of the service user in their assessments, problem formulations or interventions. She argued that in the absence of theory to underpin their practice, many social workers will consider that 'a problem is a problem' and seek to use the same interventions with all their service users (Hardman, 1997: 545). Much of the practice learning for social work students occurs with practice assessors. Trotter and Gilchrist (1996) revealed that few practice assessors or students discussed heterosexism or homophobia in supervision or provided reflection about their work with lesbian, gay, bisexual and trans (LGBT) service users in their practice curriculums. If students feel unable to discuss LGBT issues in supervision, they may be unlikely to develop competence or analyse their practice. Such students may feel ill-equipped to develop the highest standards of practice in their work both in providing support for people from LGBT communities and to maintain high standards of professional competence in risk assessment. The need for the critical analysis of social work practice is fundamental to develop best practice and also to safeguard service users from harm. This was highlighted by the case of two gay male foster carers from Wakefield who abused children in their care. The social workers in the Wakefield enquiry felt they were unable to raise concerns with their manager because they were 'afraid of being considered homophobic' (Parrott et al, 2007: 124).

In the following sections of the chapter, the usefulness of three key theoretical perspectives is examined and the benefits and limitations of each are outlined. These are: cultural competence, anti-discriminatory practice and human rights approaches.

Cultural competence

Cultural competence is an approach that originated in the US to support health professionals to provide appropriate care (Purnell, 2000). It is based on the premise that people will recover from illness and adopt healthy behaviours if the care provided takes account of the patient's cultural needs. As an approach, it has been predominantly used to inform the delivery of sensitive care with and for black and minority ethnic (BME) communities. Culturally competent practice with BME people would address issues such as the provision of interpreters, the translation of health information into languages spoken in local communities, the availability of facilities to support the religious needs of patients, appropriate diet (eg halal meat) and addressing the cultural needs of patients, such as death rituals in relation to the care of the body. Cultural competence is increasingly used as a model for religious and spiritual sensitivity in social work practice (Furness and Gilligan, 2010).

Cultural competence has also been recently developed as a framework of capabilities and principles to support social workers in their practice with lesbian, gay and bisexual people. Drawing on a range of existing models, Van Den Bergh and Crisp (2004) identify 25 principles across three domains of attitudes, knowledge and skills for the culturally competent practitioner:

■ *Attitudes*

1. Reflect on one's own sexual orientation.
2. Reflect on one's previous contact with LGBT people both personally and professionally.
3. Evaluate one's reaction to LGBT individuals, both in terms of positive and negative experiences.

4. Evaluate the cognitive, emotional and behavioural aspects of one's responses to LGBT people in order to develop awareness of potential heterosexism and homophobia.
5. Take part in personal and professional activities that foster understanding of LGBT individuals and cultures.

■ *Knowledge*

1. Key terminology related to LGBT people.
2. Demographic characteristics.
3. Intra-group diversity (ie the heterogeneity of LGBT communities).
4. Group history and traditions.
5. Group experiences of discrimination, harassment and oppression.
6. Impact of legislation and social policies.
7. Social science theories used to inform practice.
8. Community resources.
9. Culturally sensitive practice models.

■ *Skills*

1. Create an LGBT-friendly environment.
2. Assess, and not assume, service users' sexual orientation.
3. Do not assume that an individual's sexual orientation is the cause of whatever challenge an individual is facing.
4. Understand the presenting challenge holistically (in the context of their life).
5. Support service users who may be struggling with their sexual orientation.
6. Recognise indications of internalised homophobia.
7. Determine how 'out' a service user is and who supports their sexual orientation.
8. Include 'families of choice' in care plans.
9. Refer service users to LGBT community resources.
10. Obtain supervision to deal with conflicts in own value base.
11. Engage in ongoing training and continuing education around LGBT issues.

In their discussion of the model, Van Den Bergh and Crisp (2004) emphasise the need for reflection and the development of understanding of oppression and inequality in the lives of LGBT people. They discuss discrimination in housing, adoption laws and the impact of hate crimes. In their analysis, cultural competence emanated out of the activism of the gay rights movement, which lobbied for the political and social rights of citizenship.

The model is primarily concerned to achieve equality in public life and to secure the appropriateness of welfare services. Pugh (2005) discusses how assessments conducted under section 47 of the NHS and Community Care Act 1990 should take account of the cultural needs of older lesbian and gay service users. As a framework for practice, there are a number of resources which provide practical examples that can be implemented to make a difference to the delivery of services. A number of good practice guidance booklets have been developed that identify ways to be LGBT-friendly across a number of work areas (last accessed 27 February 2011 from llgbc.com). They also list local services to which social workers can refer service users.

Activity

Use the following resource to identify culturally competent social work practice in relation to: language, policies, staff training, service user involvement, information and visibility.

'How to be LGBT friendly: 30 practical ways to create a welcoming environment for LGBT people' (available at: http://www.llgbc.com/files/how_to_be_lgbt_friendly_small-2295.pdf)

Critique of cultural competence

A limitation of cultural competence as a practice model is that it may not translate well to work with LGBT communities because in popular discourse the term culture is often associated with urban spaces (Soho in London and the 'gay village' in Manchester and Birmingham) or the norms and values related to sexuality and intimacy (Pugh, 2005). This perspective emphasises common understandings that lesbian, gay and bisexual people have 'lifestyle' rather than cultural differences. The term lifestyle appears to put LGBT people's lives on the same footing as fashion, holidays and shopping, as an accessory rather than an essential to everyday life. Although the 'lifestyle' approach to lesbianism has been extensively critiqued (Kitzinger, 1987), its roots, like those of cultural competence, are in gay affirmative practice (GAP). The GAP model stems from liberal humanist approaches, which argue that LGBT people are just the same as heterosexual people: the model focuses on the individual and the internal (the notion of internalised homophobia) as opposed to the institutional and political. This is evident in the focus upon the attitudes, knowledge and skills of the individual social worker with no attention to the organisational context and the wider social and political climate in which social work is practised. Cultural competence addresses the personal and cultural aspects of people's lives but fails to consider in sufficient detail the structures in organisations and society more generally that influence how public services are delivered.

Critiques of cultural competence point to its basic assumption that if students can learn 'facts' about different cultures, their assessments will be more appropriate in people's lives (Cree and Myers, 2008). The notion that there can be facts about particular social groups and communities ignores the complexities of people's lives, risks perpetuating stereotypes and reduces individual choice if used uncritically. The underlying assumptions of the model imply that social workers with the most knowledge are best placed to work with LGBT service users. But, as with ethnicity, where black staff have been called upon to act as unofficial interpreters or consulted as the experts in 'race', there is the potential to assume that being a member of a community confers insights into the needs and experiences of a whole community. Moreover, the approach may lend itself to the over-reliance upon the goodwill of an LGBT social worker to work with LGBT communities. The approach may also be weakened by the reluctance of service users to come out to practitioners for fear of adverse responses (Charnley and Langley, 2007).

Anti-discriminatory practice

Anti-discriminatory practice (ADP) emerged as an overarching praxis to address discrimination and oppression in social work education in the late 1980s/early 1990s (Dominelli, 1988; Thompson, 1993; Dalrymple and Burke, 1995). Previously, radical social work had taken a class-based analysis based on Marxism and had failed to take full account of gender and race. ADP perspectives recognise that the achievement of social justice requires social workers to actively challenge disadvantage and empower service users to bring about change in their lives. This emphasis was partly reflected in social movements such as the Women's Liberation Movement, anti-racist organisations and disability rights movements; moreover, it was given a mandate through legislation that prohibited discrimination on the grounds of 'race', gender and disability. In parallel with the legislation, anti-discriminatory practice in social work tended to foreground 'race', gender and disability and there was less attention paid to age, religion, sexual orientation and gender identity. The regulatory body for social work, the Central Council for Education and Training in Social Work (CCETSW), explicitly required social work education to prepare students to combat discrimination. Anti-discriminatory practice was a requirement in social work training for more than a decade until the establishment of the cross-UK Care Councils in 2002.

Despite the profession's long-standing commitment to social justice, anti-discriminatory practice has been under-theorised in key social work texts (although for exceptions, see Logan et al 1996; Bayliss, 2000; Cosis Brown and Cocker, 2011). The absence of a theoretical framework for anti-discriminatory practice with LGBT people has led to a lack of clarity about oppression in their lives. Moreover, the meaning of the term 'homophobia', which is widely used to encapsulate LGBT discrimination, derives from fear, anger or disgust rather than a conceptual foundation (Fish, 2006). Recently, researchers have argued against the use of the term 'homophobia' because it emphasises individual prejudice rather than institutional, structural and cultural discrimination (Ben-Ari, 2001).

Table 3.1: Anti-discriminatory practice with LGBT people

Personal	Cultural	Structural
Attitudes	Jokes	*Historic:*
Beliefs	Stereotypes	Legislation
Feelings	Language	Medicine
Thoughts	Notions about ideal families	Social work
Actions	Assumptions that LGBT identities	*Current:*
	are sexualised	Global lack of rights

Source: Adapted from Thompson (1993).

What is heterosexism?

The oppression of lesbian, gay and bisexual people has commonly been described by the term 'homophobia'. Although the term was coined at a similar time as the term 'heterosexism', it has commonly entered the national lexicon as the term for discrimination on the grounds of sexual orientation (Fish, 2006, 2008). Heterosexism is less well understood. Herek defines heterosexism as 'societal level ideologies and patterns of institutionalized oppression of non-heterosexual people'; and homophobia as 'individual antigay attitudes and behaviour' (Herek, 2000: 19). Although this is a helpful starting point, it suggests that there are two distinct forms of discrimination and the definition does not clarify how they are related to each other. Wise (2001) coined a definition for social work that brings together personal assumptions and structural disadvantage:

> Heterosexism reflects the dominance of a worldview in which heterosexuality is used as the standard against which all people are measured ... anyone not fitting into this pattern is considered to be abnormal, morally corrupt and inferior. The assumption of heterosexuality and its superiority is perpetuated through its

institutionalization within laws, media, religions and language, which either actively discriminate against non-heterosexuals or else render them invisible though silence. Just as the concepts of racism and sexism have helped us to understand the oppression of black people and women, so the concept of heterosexism has assisted us in theorizing lesbian and gay oppression. (Wise, 2001: 154)

This definition identifies key components of oppression:

1. Heterosexuality is the norm against which lesbian, gay and bisexual people are measured (also known as heteronormativity or heterocentricity).
2. Non-heterosexual people are inferior: they are said to have biological differences and be morally depraved.
3. Heterosexuality is maintained by society's institutions including legislation, the media and religion.
4. Heterosexism shares a similar conceptual base to racism and sexism.

Towards anti-heterosexist practice in social work education

Anti-heterosexist approaches to teaching and learning seek to ensure that oppression of sexual and gender minorities is addressed throughout the learning experience:

1. Analyse existing resources to ensure that they do not perpetuate heterosexist beliefs and assumptions.
2. Develop curriculum materials and ensure discussion throughout course programmes.
3. Ensure that students have opportunities in placements to develop their practice with LGBT service users. This should include interventions assessed through practice, in direct observations, discussion in supervision, reflection, training and development.
4. Sexual orientation should not be a significant factor in risk assessment eligibility for services.
5. Reflect on unexamined assumptions, for example, about what constitutes an ideal family and the availability of role models in children's lives.
6. Consider assumptions about intimate relationships and the importance of valuing a service user's 'significant other'.
7. Understand wider influences underpinning social work practice (Bayliss, 2000).
8. Consider the impact of a life history of oppression and 'passing' (Bayliss, 2000).

9.   Review programme materials including pre-course information, interview and selection, support, consultancy, academic input, course handbook (Logan et al, 1996).
10. Creating 'safe' environments, becoming visible, the practice learning environment, practice educator training (Logan et al, 1996).

Critique of ADP approaches

ADP approaches are based on the premise that lesbian, gay, bisexual and trans people constitute a social group who experience discrimination. The term 'discrimination' means that one social group is treated less favourably than another; and, in relation to sexual orientation, the privileged group is heterosexual people. Although this perspective is important in understanding inequalities, it is limited in four key ways:

1.   In order to highlight unfair treatment, a comparison group is needed. Commonly, LGBT people as a group are compared to heterosexual people, thus emphasising the similarities between lesbian, gay and bisexual people and highlighting the differences between them and heterosexual people. The approach can inadvertently support a heteronormative framework in social work where heterosexuality is the norm against which other forms of sexuality are negatively compared. Constructing sexual categories can lead to a sexual hierarchy where good, normal and natural sexuality is associated with married (or civil partnered), monogamous, middle-class people and those outside this charmed circle are sexual deviants (Hicks, 2008). It may also lead to a fixity of sexual categories that is in contrast to people's lived experiences (eg a number of women have same-sex relationships after having been married to a man and having children).
2.   When LGBT people are described as having worse experiences of public services than heterosexual people, this could lead to unintended stereotyping and reinforce prejudice. For example, LGBT people have been described as having poorer mental health and an increased risk of suicide in comparison to heterosexual people. But this homogenises LGBT experiences and may lead to assumptions that all LGBT people have mental health problems.
3.   The emphasis upon shared experiences and characteristics emphasises similarities and ignores differences between LGBT people. Lesbians, gay men, bisexual and trans people occupy different places in the social hierarchy and are oppressed in different ways. It does not recognise that LGBT people occupy intersecting identities: for example, bisexual, disabled, female.

4. Tackling discrimination was the focus of the legislative framework (eg the Disability Discrimination Act 1995), the regulatory agenda (CCETSW, 1991) and in the role of Associated Public Bodies: the Equal Opportunities Commission (EOC), the Commission for Racial Equality (CRE) and the Disability Rights Commission (DRC). The Equality and Human Rights Commission (EHRC) has assumed the responsibilities for each of the existing equality bodies for gender, 'race' and disability. The location of the three existing equality strands in a single body alongside new responsibilities for age, religion, sexual orientation and gender identity gives a new cross-cutting focus across the seven protected grounds for reducing inequality and promoting human rights. Although human rights now underpin the delivery of public services in the UK, the approach has received relatively little attention in social work education (for an exception, see Cemlyn, 2008).

Human rights approaches

The Universal Declaration of Human Rights, which affirms that all human beings are born free and equal in dignity and rights, was adopted by the General Assembly of the United Nations in 1948 as a response to the inhumane treatment of peoples during the Second World War. The Declaration was incorporated into UK legislation by the Human Rights Act 1998 and is embedded in public services and social institutions.

What are human rights?

Human rights are basic entitlements to fair and dignified treatment and are obtained by everyone simply because they are human beings. They are based on the five core principles of fairness, respect, equality, dignity and autonomy, commonly known by the acronym FREDA (Fish and Bewley, 2010). Human rights impact on people's everyday lives by protecting their freedom to have control over their own lives and help to ensure fair and equal services from public bodies.

Human rights legislation marks a shift from basic civil and political rights to include social, economic and cultural rights and the state's duty to provide for its citizens. Cemlyn (2008) argues that human rights include the notions of distributive justice and multilayered citizenship. Human rights are fundamental to social work practice: being safe and protected from harm, being treated fairly and with dignity, having autonomy, and taking an active role in local communities and wider society. They underpin work in child protection and safeguarding adults, they mean that people with disabilities should have access to independent living arrangements and have choice and control in their lives through, for example, direct payments or individual budgets. They also mean that people should have a say in the way that services are delivered and be able to ensure that public bodies are held to account for the ways that services are planned and accessed.

Human rights as a global approach to social work

Human rights are increasingly central to the global practice of social work. In 2010, the International Federation of Social Workers (IFSW) and the International Association of Schools of Social Work (IASSW) signalled their commitment to making human rights principles integral to the practice of social work and the education of social work students. The approach enables practitioners, academics and students to identify international social justice concerns and to see the links between them.

Social workers practise alongside people who are among the most disadvantaged in society to promote change in their lives, support them to find solutions to problems and enhance their well-being. They seek to empower people to address personal and social difficulties and obtain resources and services to meet their needs. The case for human rights in social work was outlined by the United Nations in 1994:

> More than many professionals, social work educators and practitioners are conscious that their concerns are closely linked to respect for human rights. They accept the premise that human rights and fundamental freedoms are indivisible and that the full realisation of civil and political rights are impossible without enjoyment of economic, social and cultural rights. They believe that the achievement of lasting progress in the implementation of human rights depends on effective national and international policies of economic and social development. Their direct knowledge of the vulnerable sectors of society makes social work educators and practitioners valuable in the formulation of social policies. (Centre for Human Rights, 1994)

Social workers have a responsibility to ensure that people are safe, have their rights protected and are able to exercise choice and control. These are necessary to ensuring that people receive the highest standards of social

Table 3.2: The relevance of human rights to social work practice

Human right	Relevant issues in social work
The right not to be treated in an inhuman or degrading way *Inhuman treatment means treatment causing severe mental or physical suffering* *Degrading treatment means treatment that is grossly humiliating or undignified*	Safeguarding adults from physical, financial or mental abuse Safeguarding children from physical, sexual and emotional abuse or neglect Soiled unchanged sheets in care homes Leaving trays of food without helping a disabled person or an older person to eat when they are unable to feed themselves Excessive force used to restrain service users
The right to respect for private and family life, home and correspondence *Family life is interpreted broadly. It does not cover just blood or formalised relationships and includes the family life of LGBT people (Williams, 2001)* *Private life includes issues such as personal choices, relationships, physical and mental well-being, access to personal information and participation in community life*	Privacy in care homes Family visits Sexual and other relationships Participation in social and recreational activities Personal records Independent living Closure of residential care homes Separation of families due to residential care placements
The right to liberty *The right to liberty is not a right to be free to do whatever you want. The right to liberty is a right not to be deprived of liberty in an arbitrary manner* *The right to liberty is a limited right. It can be limited in a number of specific circumstances, for example, the lawful detention of someone who has mental health issues*	Informal detention of service users who do not have the capacity to decide whether they would like to be admitted to hospital, for example, those with Alzheimer's disease Delays in reviewing whether mental health users who are detained under the Mental Health Act should still be detained or delays in discharge Excessive restraint (putting someone with learning difficulties in a wheelchair for long periods of time)
The right not to be discriminated against *This is not a free-standing right but relates to the entitlement to the rights contained in the Human Rights Act 1998* *Discrimination takes place when someone is treated in a different way compared with someone else in a similar situation* *Indirect discrimination happens when someone is treated in the same way as others that does not take into account the person's different situation. A distinction in treatment must be reasonably and objectively justified*	Non-English speakers being presented with a care package without the use of an interpreter

Source: Adapted from DH (2008a).

care. A human rights approach emphasises the importance of involving people and pays attention to how they are treated. Values are at the heart of social work practice and education. At the 2010 international conference, the IFSW and IASSW launched a joint website to inform the teaching of human rights and to embed the approach in social work practice (see http:// www.ifsw.org/p38001792.html).

Congress (2006) proposed a five-step ETHIC (Examine, Think, Hypothesise, Identify, Consult) model, which could enable social workers to make decisions quickly in their day-to-day practice:

■ *Examine* – students begin by examining themselves and understanding how their own value systems, as well as cultural and societal values, may affect their attitudes and behaviours and the decisions that they make about clients. Students are also expected to examine client and agency values, and finally to look at how professional values can guide and shape their decision about a specific ethical dilemma.

■ *Think* about the Universal Declaration of Human Rights and related covenants, as well as the national social work association's code of ethics, relevant laws and agency regulations. Students are asked to examine all ethical dilemmas in the context of the Universal Declaration and their own national codes and relevant legislation. Finally, social workers must understand the agency context including statutes and regulations that may impact on ethical decision-making.

■ *Hypothesise* different courses of action based on varied decisions. Students are asked to develop scenarios based on different decisions about ethical dilemmas to help them decide between alternative courses of action.

■ *Identify* who is the most vulnerable and who will be harmed or helped in terms of social work's commitment to the most vulnerable. More than other professions, social work is concerned about the most vulnerable and the most disadvantaged in societies around the world.

■ *Consult* with supervisors and colleagues, both within and outside the agency. It is essential that students learn the importance of consulting with others, especially around challenging ethical issues, as they progress in their professional careers (see Congress, 2006: 9–10).

Human rights approaches in social work

The principles of human rights and social justice are fundamental to social work both globally and nationally (Centre for Human Rights, 1994). Human rights discourses are reflected in the UK Quality Assurance Agency for Higher Education (QAA) benchmark statement for social work, which includes a commitment to protect the rights of service users and understand the impact of injustice, social inequalities and oppressive social relations (QAA, 2008). Human rights principles also form part of the performance criteria of the National Occupational Standards for Social Work which students must meet to demonstrate their competence on placement, for example:

■ acknowledge people as citizens and respect their human rights (TOPSS, 2002: 30);
■ know about legislation, policy and procedural requirements and associated human rights (TOPSS, 2002: 55);
■ be aware of sources of knowledge that will assist you when working with ethical and human rights dilemmas (TOPSS, 2002: 60).

The code of practice for social workers draws upon the concepts and values of human rights perspectives, including (GSCC, 2010: 13):

1.1   Treating each person as an individual;
1.2   Respecting and, where appropriate, promoting the individual views and wishes of both service users and carers;
1.3   Supporting service users' rights to control their lives and make informed choices about the services they receive;
1.4   Respecting and maintaining the dignity and privacy of service users;
1.5   Promoting equal opportunities for service users and carers; and
1.6   Respecting diversity and different cultures and values …
3.1   Promoting the independence of service users and assisting them to understand and exercise their rights.

This emphasis on how service users are treated is reflected in the focus on social work ethics; the approach seeks to involve service users in decisions that directly affect them, supporting them to live healthy and independent lives, and also in shaping the delivery of services (SCIE, 2003). Williams (2001) argues that the Human Rights Act 1998 may potentially have a greater impact on UK social work practice than other major pieces of legislation including the Children Act 1989 and the NHS and Community Care Act 1990. In contrast to previous equality legislation where the burden of proof lay with the defendant to show that discrimination had occurred (and was thus reactive), current legislation places a positive duty on public services (and voluntary-sector organisations and charities with a public service function) to ensure equality and fairness for all (and is thus proactive).

Human rights and LGBT people

In many countries, LGBT people do not enjoy the rights and freedoms contained in the Universal Declaration. In 76 UN member states, consensual same-sex behaviour among adults is criminalised and often leads to imprisonment, as in the case of a highly publicised gay male couple in Malawi. (In the jurisdictions of many countries, it is specifically gay men who are penalised.) In five countries, same-sex behaviour is punishable by the death penalty. In 2010, the government of Uganda sought to introduce an anti-homosexuality bill, which would introduce the death penalty for same-sex behaviour, and life imprisonment or a prison sentence of seven years for anyone who encouraged same-sex behaviour (see http://www.guardian.co.uk/commentisfree/belief/2011/may/11/uganda-anti-gay-bill).

The framework of human rights has contributed to challenging violations in people's freedoms and has brought about the achievement of unprecedented rights and freedoms for LGBT people internationally (see Ottosson, 2010):

- the legalisation of same-sex behaviour (115 countries)
- equal age of consent (99 countries)
- prohibition of discrimination in employment (49 countries)
- prohibition of discrimination in the state constitution (9 countries)
- recognition of hate crimes on the grounds of sexual orientation (17 countries)
- recognition of hate crimes on the grounds of gender identity (3 countries)
- incitement to hatred (20 countries)
- same-sex marriage (7 countries)
- marriage-like status (civil partnerships, civil unions, etc) (11 countries)
- joint adoption by same-sex couples (10 countries)
- gender recognition after gender reassignment (16 countries).

Human rights principles have underpinned a number of successful challenges to the abuse of rights and freedoms in the European Union (EU) in areas including: EU anti-discrimination law; attitudes towards LGBT people; freedom of assembly; hate crime and hate speech; the labour market; education; media; healthcare; religious institutions; asylum; multiple discrimination; and trans people (FRA, 2009).

The Yogykarta principles, which constitute a global charter for LGBT human rights, include calls for the decriminalisation of sexual orientation in countries across the world and recognition of same-sex relationships by state governments (International Service for Human Rights, 2007).

In 2009, the United Nations General Assembly issued a statement to confirm that human rights protections include sexual orientation and gender identity and condemned human rights abuses against LGBT people.

Human rights: a new agenda for social work?

There are a number of myths about human rights that have often been perpetuated by the media. There are beliefs that human rights give better protection for criminals than for ordinary people, that they make people less safe, and that human rights abuses are an issue for other countries and do not occur in the UK (EHRC, 2008). Such critiques have also been extended to social work. Although little attention has been directed to the impact that human rights have had on the lives of people who are socially excluded, it is possibly too early to say that legislation has failed to transform social care services (Clements, no date). A human rights approach to the delivery of social care recognises that people are key actors rather than passive recipients of services (Calma, 2008). Human rights have underpinned the Shaping Our Lives initiative, which will see the transfer of decision-making to users of services in the form of personal and direct payments budgets (Beresford, no date).

Human rights are universal and indivisible and they help to acknowledge the global dimension in which social work is practised. In an address to the joint IFSW and IASSW conference in Montreal, Jim Ife (2001: 5) argued that a global perspective must be part of the everyday practice of social workers because 'all aspects of social work are affected by global issues and all social problems have a global dimension'. He proposed that human rights are central to the pursuit of social justice and work towards living in one world:

> the key value bases of social work ... can best be articulated through a human rights perspective.... Human rights are constructed as the consequence of on-going dialogue about what is important for all the people of the world, and what constitutes the important elements of our common humanity and our global citizenship. (Ife, 2001: 10)

The challenge for social work is to develop theoretical formulations of human rights and identify practice examples.

Exercise

In the 2010 National Cancer Patient Experience Survey a question was asked about a patient's sexual orientation for the first time. This annual survey of over 100,000 patients monitors progress on cancer care and provides important preliminary evidence about LGBT people's experiences of cancer services (a question was not asked about gender identity). Analysis showed significant differences in the experiences of cancer services between LGBT and heterosexual patients, where LGBT patients reported less positive views in relation to 16 questions (DH, 2010b: 99):

- Got understandable answers from the Clinical Nurse Specialist all/most of the time
- Time spent with the Clinical Nurse Specialist was about right
- Patient was given information about support/self help groups for people with cancer
- Received understandable answers from hospital doctor on important questions the patient had asked
- Doctors never talked in front of patient as if they were not there
- Received understandable answers from ward nurses on important questions the patient had asked
- Ward nurses never talked in front of patient as if they were not there
- Doctors/nurses never deliberately did not tell patient things they wanted to know
- Never received conflicting information from doctors or nurses
- Hospital staff always did everything they could to control their pain
- Always treated with respect and dignity by hospital staff
- Staff definitely did everything they could to control side effects of chemotherapy
- Staff definitely did all they could in outpatients/day case to control the patient's pain
- Definitely given enough emotional support from hospital staff in outpatients/day case
- GP staff definitely did everything they could to support the patient whilst they were having cancer treatment
- Never felt treated as a set of cancer symptoms rather than as a whole person.

Question
Use the human rights principles of freedom, respect, equality, dignity and autonomy to reflect on the differences in the ways patients were treated.

Further reading

Beresford, P. (no date) *Access to Social Care: Shaping Our Lives. Human Rights: Transforming Services*, London: SCIE. Available at: www.scie.org.uk (accessed 8 September 2010).

Calma, T. (2008) 'The role of social workers as human rights workers with Indigenous people and communities', Australian Human Rights Commission. Available at: http://www.hreoc.gov.au/about/media/speeches/social_justice/2008/20080212_socialwork.html (accessed 8 September 2010).

Clements, L. (no date) *Access to Justice: Human Rights Poverty and Social Exclusion. Human Rights: Transforming Services*, London: SCIE. Available at: www.scie.org.uk (accessed 8 September 2010).

DH (Department of Health) (2010b) *National Cancer Patient Experience Survey*, London: Department of Health.

FRA (EU Fundamental Rights Agency) (2009) 'Homophobia and discrimination on grounds of sexual orientation and gender identity in the EU member states'. Available at: http://www.fra.europa.eu/fraWebsite/attachments/FRA_hdgso_report_Part%202_en.pdf (accessed 2 September 2010).

Ife, J. (2001) 'Local and global practice: relocating social work as a human rights profession in the new global order', *European Journal of Social Work*, 4, 5–15.

Luft, J. and Ingham, H. (1955) 'The Johari window, a graphic model of interpersonal awareness', Proceedings of the western training laboratory in group development, Los Angeles: University of California at Los Angeles.

Parrott, B., McIver, A. and Thoburn, J. (2007) 'Independent Inquiry Report into the circumstances of Child Sexual Abuse by two Foster Carers in Wakefield'. Available at: www.wakefield.gov.uk (accessed 8 September 2010).

Trans people in social work

Practice scenario

Nicole ... she's a transwoman, she was sectioned ... I am sure the hospital ward itself is quite nice down there, it's quite nicely laid out. But there was no sense of trying to make her feel comfortable as a trans person ... because she was sectioned she wasn't allowed a razor which means ultimately she was growing a beard whilst in there. And I think that sort of atmosphere just made her look in the mirror, feel bad, she got worse, and it was a kind of spiraling thing. I don't think there was any acknowledgement whatsoever by the staff towards her being a transwoman. (Willis et al, 2011)

Questions

Drawing on the material in this chapter, consider the following questions to develop your understanding of the potential issues facing Nicole as a user of social work services:

- In what ways could staff on this mental health ward acknowledge Nicole's identity as a trans woman?
- What legal protections are afforded to trans people as users of public services?
- Identify potential discrimination on the grounds of gender identity in social work and other public services.

Introduction

Trans people have only recently been recognised as users of health and social care services (DH, 2008c). In comparison to lesbian, gay and bisexual people, they have been almost totally overlooked in social work theory or research (Kenagy, 2005; Davis, 2008; Alleyn and Jones, 2010). Previous studies have sometimes included trans people in their samples, but have failed to give separate consideration of their specific concerns. Existing research has focused largely on four main areas: theoretical understandings about sex and gender (Ekins and King, 1997; Kessler and McKenna, 2000); biomedical research (Feldman and Bockting, 2001); and, more recently, research into the barriers to accessing gender reassignment services; and policy-oriented work (Xavier et al, 2007). Knowledge about trans people's access to social care services is often drawn from small-scale studies and narrative accounts (Davis, 2008).

Underpinning knowledge

Conceptual issues: understanding sex and gender

Sex is considered to be a defining and enduring aspect of who we are. We think of it as unambiguous: the distinctions between the sexes are thought to be clear-cut with physical and biological characteristics that differentiate men and women. These sex differences are often believed to correspond to gender attributes; that is, the psychological, emotional and social roles associated with being female and male. Women and men are also believed to be distinguished from each other by their clothes, voice pitch, mannerisms and topics of conversation. Historically, these beliefs were so widely held that different jobs were deemed suitable for men (coalminer) and women (secretary). Moreover, the biological ability to have babies was associated with the social role of bringing up children. Although this binary system (man–woman; male–female) is sometimes unsettled by individuals who step out of traditional expectations about gender roles (a male nurse or a female firefighter), there is a persistent belief that there are only two genders and that one's sex and one's gender match up with societal beliefs about them (a person with a woman's body will perceive themselves as female and vice versa). Gender identity refers to an individual's self-perception as female or male; however, some people perceive themselves as having both female and male characteristics or to be outside of traditional ideas about sex and gender. Sex differences are fundamental to everyday life in the UK and many public services are organised along gender lines, including hospital wards, prisons and some mental health services.

Who are trans people?

The terms trans and transgender are overarching terms used to describe people who are gender variant including people who are cross-dressers or transvestites (people who wear clothing often associated with the opposite gender), transsexual people (those who undergo gender reassignment to live permanently in their acquired gender), third gender or androgyne people (those who do not identify as male or female) and intersex people (those born with the physical characteristics of both sexes). Trans is therefore an inclusive term that embraces people who do not live full-time in their preferred gender because:

> the casual onlooker may not be able to distinguish between someone who identifies as a cross-dresser/transvestite and is 'dressed' and someone who is living full-time in their acquired gender. They are also not discrete groups.... Today's cross-dresser can become tomorrow's transsexual and regardless of how an individual identifies, they can be equally vulnerable in public spaces. (Whittle et al, 2007: 94)

Trans describes people who transgress gender boundaries without necessarily having surgery. Trans people may access hormone and other treatments and choose not to undergo surgery. The waiting times for surgery are lengthy and many people feel they are suspended in limbo as they access treatment through the NHS. The process of changing gender is known as *transitioning*; someone who is transitioning from female to male (FTM) is often known as a *trans man*, while male to female (MTF) transsexual people are known as *trans women*. After successfully transitioning to live permanently in their preferred gender role, many prefer to be considered simply as men or women. Trans people can be heterosexual, lesbian, gay or bisexual.

Gender identity and gender reassignment

Transsexual is a medicalised term that describes people who seek gender reassignment treatments including genital reconstructive surgery, hormone treatments and voice coaching. Before clinical intervention is offered, the intending transitioner must live as a person of the intended gender for a period of a year. This is known as the 'Real Life Test', which demonstrates the ability to integrate socially in the acquired gender role. In order to achieve social integration, trans people need to feel a sense of authenticity by 'passing' and being accepted by others. Medical professionals in gender identity clinics require a high degree of conformity to traditional gender roles in order to distinguish 'real' candidates (those who will subsequently receive surgery) from others. These assessments evaluate whether candidates are, for example, 'real women' in such areas as relationships with men, interest in and caring for children, and the capacity to work continuously in female occupations. One of the reasons (some) transsexuals may seem to conform to stereotyped female appearance and behaviour in the wearing of make-up and frilly, feminine clothes is that they have to prove to psychiatrists that they can pass as women.

The notion of 'real' women or men is discriminatory; it refers to the idea that only people who are born women are real. It sets up a hierarchy that classifies people who become women as less entitled to female status; this is often manifested in a refusal to accept the person's name in their acquired gender: 'I have a few jerks in work that think its [sic] amusing to call me over the tannoy using my former name' (Whittle et al, 2007: 37).

Gender identity was also at the centre of the 2009 Olympic gold medal win of South African athlete, Caster Semenya, who was subjected to unwarranted questions about her gender and obliged to prove she is a woman through a gender verification test (Kessel, 2009).

Gender nonconformity

New theoretical understandings have enabled a conceptual shift from pathology (ie gender dysphoria or disorder) to gender nonconformity (not conforming to society's narrow view about gender) (Fish, 2006).

In order to access gender reassignment treatments, the person must have a diagnosis of Gender Identity Disorder (GID), which is listed as a mental health problem in the Diagnostic and Statistical Manual (DSM) IV of the American Psychiatric Association (APA) and the World Health Organisation's International Classification of Diseases: ICD-10. Gender dysphoria is the term used by psychiatrists and psychologists to describe the unease that transsexual people have about the gender they were assigned at birth. The diagnosis of gender dysphoria is:

> characterised by a strong and persistent cross–gender identification which does not arise from a desire to obtain the cultural advantages of being the other sex and that it should not be confused with simple nonconformity to stereotypical sex role behaviour. (Whittle et al, 2008: 9)

Work is being undertaken leading to the issue of DSM V and ICD-11 and a number of trans service users have lobbied for the removal of GID from the psychiatric classification. There are concerns that the removal of GID as a diagnostic category may result in the discontinuation of publicly funded services (di Ceglie, 2010).

Internationally, standards of care are determined by the World Professional Association for Transgender Health (WPATH). Many trans people consider them as gatekeeping access to treatment.

Experiences of discrimination and harassment

Trans people meet with discrimination and prejudice in their everyday lives (Grant et al, 2010). This places limits on their employment opportunities, despite legislation prohibiting discrimination; their personal relationships; their access to goods, services and housing; their health status; and their access to health and social care. Harassment in public spaces is common: a Europe-wide study found that 79% of survey respondents had experienced some form of harassment ranging from transphobic comments to physical or sexual abuse (Turner et al, 2009). Ordinary activities, such as use of leisure facilities, may not be accessible for trans people because they fear discrimination in changing rooms or single-sex sports provision (Whittle et al, 2007). Many, regardless of social position, experience isolation and face limited understanding of their lives. These experiences place many trans people at risk of alcohol abuse, depression, suicide and self-harm, violence, and substance abuse (Kenagy, 2005).

In the largest UK study of trans people to date, Whittle et al (2007) found that almost 29% had experienced verbal harassment or name-calling at work; in a Brighton study, some were working below their capacity or denied promotion:

> In my current job I think I'm being kind of unfairly discriminated against for the purpose of promotion … they're worried … as to how the customers will react if I have a position over of authority, if they were to call a manager to solve the situation and the manager is trans, I think that's where they're kind of really concerned, and because of that I'm being treated worse. (Browne and Lim, 2008b: 32)

Despite legislation prohibiting discrimination, some were unable to maintain their employment because of harassment from colleagues:

> I finally threw the towel in at work (civil service) because of almost five years of harassment and discrimination. I was left for months, unable to use male or female toilets because no one liked it and warned off wearing 'frocks' to work! My employer, an equal opportunities employer, could not offer me a job free from harassment anywhere. (Whittle et al, 2007: 37)

Some employers have developed equality policies that include trans people and take their responsibilities seriously to support them during gender transition:

> One day my boss just called me into his office and said, 'there's no easy way to say this: are you going for a sex change?' I thought I was going to get a P45, but I wasn't really going to live a lie anymore, so I said 'Yes'. He just said 'Get a letter from your GP saying you're undergoing gender reassignment, we'll support you 100%'. That's because a policy had just been developed and had addressed trans issues following legislation. (Browne and Lim, 2008b: 33)

In a survey of 96 public-sector organisations, 23% said they had noted an improvement in trans equality but that in terms of setting specific trans equality actions and achieving outcomes to meet the general and specific public-sector equality duties, there was still a considerable way to go (Rankin et al, 2010).

Policy and legislation

In the mid–1990s, a number of trans activists formed a social and political movement that sought equal rights and anti-discrimination legislation. More recently, legislative developments in Europe have also influenced the rights and protections afforded in the UK.

1999 Sex Discrimination (Gender Reassignment) Regulations

The 1975 Sex Discrimination Act (SDA) did not provide protection from discrimination for transsexual people. Following a European Court ruling, the 1999 regulations amended the SDA and offered protection for transsexual people against discrimination in employment and vocational training. The scope of the legislation provided protection for those who are intending to undergo gender reassignment, are in the process of reassignment or have already undergone gender reassignment.

2004 Gender Recognition Act

This legislation gives trans people legal recognition for their acquired gender, including marriage, and allows them to obtain a new birth certificate. The Act includes measures that protect trans people's right to privacy about their birth status and current identity.

Section 22 of the 2004 Gender Recognition Act (GRA) makes it illegal for any individual who has obtained information in an official capacity to divulge that someone is a trans person with a gender recognition certificate.

This includes social and health care agencies, or a person employed by such an agency or prospective agency.

2005 Gender Recognition (Exceptions to Offence of Disclosure) Order

This order creates an exception to section 22 of the GRA for health and social care professionals where the person making the disclosure has a reasonable belief that:

- either consent has been given or that consent cannot be given by that person; and
- the disclosure is made to a health professional for medical purposes.

2008 Sex Discrimination (Amendment of Legislation) Regulations

These regulations provide protection against discrimination and harassment on the grounds of gender reassignment in goods, facilities and services. Excluded matters include education (including vocational training); the content of media and advertisements; and the provision of goods, facilities or services at a place occupied or used for the purposes of an organised religion.

2010 Single Equality Act and gender identity

Gender identity will be treated as a protected characteristic alongside eight other grounds. The legislation includes specific provisions of relevance for trans people. It will include:

- changing the definition of gender reassignment by removing the requirement for medical supervision;
- extending Public Sector Equality Duties to include gender reassignment; and
- including prohibition on discrimination against those who are associated with trans people.

Gender Recognition Panel

The criteria for legal status afforded by the Gender Recognition Panel (GRP) means that the trans person must show that they have been diagnosed as having gender dysphoria and that they have lived in their acquired gender role for two years and intend to do so permanently for the remainder of their life. In order to obtain a Gender Recognition Certificate, a person does not have to have had gender reassignment surgery.

Political organising

Although the trans community is relatively 'young' (Whittle et al, 2008) because access to gender reassignment services has only been possible since the 1960s, being trans is not a recent phenomenon. Historical figures known to be trans include James Barry (a British surgeon born in 1795); Billy Tipton, the musician; Jan Morris, the writer; Renee Richards, the sportswoman; and Jan Hamilton, who served as a paratrooper during the Iraq war.

Political activism in trans communities emerged alongside lesbian, gay and bisexual (LGB) activism in the Stonewall rebellion against police brutality in the late 1960s. The relationship between LGB and trans people has at times been an uneasy one, with many trans people feeling that the concerns differ significantly. The inclusion of trans issues under the rubric of LGBT conveys the mistaken impression that trans people's concerns primarily relate to sexual orientation and that being trans is 'an extreme form of homosexuality' (Whittle et al, 2008: 51). Although there are similar experiences where health care and other professionals lack awareness and understanding, LGB people's identities are no longer medicalised and they do not rely on a medical diagnosis to achieve their identities (Whittle et al, 2008: 51).

The demographics of trans communities

There are no official figures for the UK trans population: the Census does not include questions about trans status; moreover, no major government surveys collect information about trans people. Since the GRP was established in 2005, 2,500 people have successfully applied to have their acquired gender legally acknowledged (GRP, 2010). However, twice this number had applied to the Home Office by 2000 to have their passport changed. The numbers of people who seek legal recognition are likely to form a small proportion of the overall trans population and other estimates have ranged from 65,000 (Johnson, 2005) to 300,000 (Reed et al, 2009).

The evidence is complex in relation to income and social class. In comparison to the general population, trans people are more likely to be employed in managerial and professional occupations (Whittle et al, 2007). Yet they are also likely to be located at the lower end of salary scales; in one UK study, trans people were three times more likely than LGB people to have an annual income of less than £10,000 and they were also less likely to be in full-time employment (Browne and Lim, 2008b). Across Europe, almost half of trans people earn less than average salaries (Turner et al, 2009). These findings may be explained by experiences of workplace discrimination: at the point of transitioning, trans people are more likely to face harassment in the workplace, dismissal or a change in their working conditions (Whittle et al, 2007). Although recent legislation offers protection for trans people in the workplace, many organisations do not have policies and procedures to support someone in their gender transition.

Two thirds of trans people in the UK identify as female (Browne and Lim, 2008b) and these proportions are similar in Denmark, France, Holland, Finland and Hungary. By contrast, in Germany, Greece and Italy, trans people are more likely to identify as male. In Sweden, the proportions are equal (Turner et al, 2009). In comparison to LGB people, trans people are more likely to be parents or closely related to a child (Browne and Lim, 2008b).

Access to social care

Access to gender reassignment services has been the most pressing research concern (Schonfield, 2008); consequently, practice knowledge in social care with trans people is lacking. In a survey of 400 social care services conducted by the Commission for Social Care Inspection (CSCI, 2008), only six services had undertaken work on gender identity. In every case, this was in response to a trans person using the service. The following sections draw upon a small body of largely unpublished work which identifies trans people's needs in social care, including: transphobic hate crime, housing and homelessness, mental health, domestic abuse, older trans people and residential care homes, and trans self-help groups. Trans people may be users of every aspect of social care services.

Transphobic hate crime

Every person has the right to go into public spaces without fear of attack or harassment; it is fundamental to feeling part of a community and being safe within it. Human rights legislation offers protection from violence and abuse and the right to liberty and security. Following the death of Stephen Lawrence, there has been increasing recognition that members of minority groups are at risk of hate crimes and legislation has been introduced to protect people on the grounds of 'race' and disability. Hate crimes differ from other offences because they are motivated by the perpetrator's hostility towards the victim's identity or perceived identity.

New provisions introduced by the Criminal Justice and Immigration Act 2008 (and implemented in 2010) create an offence of intentionally stirring up hatred on the grounds of sexual orientation. The new offences deal with conduct (either words or behaviour) or material that is threatening in nature, and which is intended to stir up hatred. The Crown Prosecution Service (CPS) and the Association of Chief Police Officers (ACPO) have agreed five monitored strands of hate crime, and these are:

- disability;
- race;
- religion or belief;
- sexual orientation;
- transgender identity (see cps.gov.uk).

The legislation builds on section 146 of the Criminal Justice Act 2003, which imposed a duty on courts to increase a sentence for any offence aggravated by prejudice based on sexual orientation. The CPS issued guidance that extends hate crimes to cases where the offence is perpetrated against a trans person (CPS, 2009). The policy aims to give a clear message that hate crimes are unacceptable and that offences will be treated seriously and encourages trans people to report them. High levels of physical and verbal abuse are experienced by trans people in public spaces: the majority (73%) of trans people had experienced 'comments, threatening behaviour, physical abuse, verbal abuse or sexual abuse' (Whittle et al, 2007: 53). They noted that 27% of respondents who live in their acquired gender permanently said they had not experienced abuse (despite incidents of robbery and muggings) because they believed they effectively 'pass' in their acquired gender. The researchers suggested that some trans people may have built up a 'personal story over many years of better passing than is reality' (Whittle et al, 2007: 53) and they argue that the 27% is an under-reporting. These findings are supported by a study of 2,669 trans people conducted across Europe where 79% of respondents reported some form of harassment in public spaces ranging from comments to physical or sexual abuse (Turner et al, 2009). They were twice as likely to have been victims of physical violence and three times as likely to experience harassment as LGB people (Browne and Lim, 2008b). The lack of safety in public spaces and the risk of social exclusion are concerns for trans people.

Housing and homelessness

In comparison to the UK population as a whole, twice as many trans people live in the private rented sector where tenure is less secure and of poorer quality (Whittle et al, 2007). Living in private-sector accommodation affords less protection and trans people are vulnerable to the prejudices of landlords. Housing is an ongoing concern: they are less likely to be happy with their accommodation and to own their own home (Whittle et al, 2007; Browne and Lim, 2008b). In Brighton, researchers found that participants were more likely to live in social housing and encounter problems in finding accommodation; over a third had been homeless at some stage in their lives (Browne and Lim, 2008b). Also, a study in Scotland found that 25% of research participants had to leave their family home due to the transphobic reactions of their families, housemates or neighbours (STA, 2008). Research suggests that trans people lose their family support networks and feel excluded from their local community following transition (Whittle et al, 2007).

Domestic abuse

The Scottish Transgender Alliance (STA) conducted the first study that focused solely on trans people's experiences of domestic abuse (Roche et al, 2010). Sixty people took part in the online survey and seven qualitative interviews were undertaken. The findings suggested high levels of domestic abuse with 80% of survey respondents reporting emotional, physical or sexual abuse from a current or former partner based on a rejection of their trans identity. Almost half had experienced controlling behaviours including restricting the clothes worn and limiting access to joint finances. Many said that partners made derogatory comments that made them feel worthless.

The study suggested that many trans people have 'smaller and less supportive' social circles as a result of their trans status (Roche et al, 2010: 28). They have a strong awareness of the potential for transphobic reactions, which means that they often avoid close social relationships; some described themselves as private individuals who had grown up with few friends because they experienced gender discomfort as children. Respondents were sometimes isolated and, as a result, did not recognise the experience as abusive and lacked confidence to seek support:

> It was only when the relationship broke up that I realised it was wrong. At the time I did not consider myself oppressed. I thought it was wrong to be transgender and so could understand why it upset her so much. (Roche et al, 2010: 29)

Just over half had contacted a friend, relative or neighbour, while very few (7%) contacted specialist domestic abuse services and 25% did not tell anyone. They expected that service providers would not treat them with respect:

> Didn't want to tell any service providers about the relationship problems as explaining the details would have required me to come out … I was worried service providers would be ignorant of trans identities and potentially even quite prejudiced. (Roche et al, 2010: 29)

A Brighton study, which also included lesbian, gay and bisexual people, revealed that trans people are more likely to experience domestic abuse than their LGB counterparts (64% versus 29%) (Browne and Lim, 2008a).

Mental health

More than one in three of respondents in the 'Engendered penalties' study said they had attempted suicide at least once as an adult (Whittle et al, 2007). Moreover, they are more likely to report that they have poor emotional and mental health than LGB respondents (Browne and Lim, 2008a). Trans people felt strongly that their mental health problems were not caused by their gender identity, but by the lack of social support, isolation and transphobic responses in everyday life. Some felt that the medicalisation of trans identities and the diagnosis of GID reduces their autonomy and labels them as mentally ill (Browne and Lim, 2008a).

Older trans people and residential care homes

Johnson (2005) contacted 150 agencies in health and social care and this work informed her report on residential and community care for trans people. She identifies 24 good practice guidelines for care providers including the recruitment and training of staff in trans issues, policies and practices to meet the needs of trans people, developing links with trans organisations in the community, and the right to be treated in a non–discriminatory way. She also identified issues relevant for social workers, social care providers and inspection teams from the Care Quality Commission (Johnson, 2005: 10):

- ensure that assessment procedures and processes incorporate trans concerns;
- make available necessary information to clients of care services to enable them to make personal choices;
- ensure that trans projects are supported not only in terms of financial concerns, but also other broader resource issues, for example, training opportunities;
- establish and maintain fruitful relationships with trans projects;

■ review their terms and conditions of funding to be aware of the possibility of the abuse of trans projects;

■ ensure that social services inspection teams are aware of and understand trans needs and allow lay assessors to be involved with inspection teams.

In recent years, reminiscence has been used as a therapeutic tool to promote the mental and emotional well-being of older people. For many older people, reminiscence work can help them feel less alone with their memories and can bring resolution by sharing experiences in a group or in one-to-one sessions. Some trans people may have chosen not to talk about their earlier life and may have painful memories (Johnson, 2005). It may be appropriate for social workers to discuss the content of sessions with the trans service user before undertaking group work and to work with the other group members about trans issues.

Developing good practice in assessments of need and risk

Initial assessments with trans people should include assessing social supports including friends, family of origin, chosen family, relationship to the trans community and professional supports. Holman and Goldberg (2006) consider immediate risks to health and safety and routinely assess grief and loss:

> It has been our experience that trans people and loved ones have often experienced multiple losses related to societal transphobia, including family/community rejection following disclosure of being trans or the loved one of a trans person, as well as loss of work and housing. (Holman and Goldberg, 2006: 3)

In order to build a holistic assessment, it is important to identify strengths to sustain and enhance a service user's sense of competency and agency. Many trans people have been refused services and, prior to making a referral, it is important to contact the agency to ensure the accessibility of the service for trans people (Holman and Goldberg, 2006).

Trans self-help groups

Dissatisfaction with existing provision means that caregiving is undertaken within the 'social circle that exists around the care-recipient' (Johnson, 2005: 7). Community ties may need to be forged anew as people often move to a different locality following transition. Self-help groups have been set up to fill the gaps in care and address the specificities of trans people's practices of care: affirming a positive identity, alleviating isolation and offering advice and information (Hines, 2007). Sharing experiences was often seen as a way of giving something back to the community.

Good practice guidance

The Adult and Community Services Directorate within Lancashire County Council commissioned a programme of training provided by a trans organisation for physical disability and sensory impairment direct care staff, ancillary and administration staff, and managers across Lancashire.

What was the outcome?

Staff who are commissioned to work with disabled and or older trans people are much more confident in supporting them, particularly in relation to situations involving safeguarding issues, rehabilitation, self-directed support, personalised budgets, writing care plans and in providing personal and intimate care. Disabled and or older trans service users feel that better consideration is given to maintaining their dignity because staff show respect for their gender identity by enabling them to express it.

Some trans people have physical or learning disabilities that mean they require assistance with personal care. The freedom to express identity through choice of clothing is something that many people take for granted, but it can be very difficult to achieve for a disabled trans person if they need help from other people to get dressed, or to purchase and choose their clothing.

Disabled trans people may also find it harder to know how other people perceive their gender presentation. For example, if someone is partially sighted they may need additional support from social care workers to find a way to convey more easily their gender identity through their choice of clothes and hairstyle.

Often social care workers providing personal care to a disabled service user are expected to be of the same gender as the service user. This can result in staff allocation issues if a disabled service user wishes to start gender reassignment or lives in more than one gender role (EHRC, 2007a: 25).

Conclusion: social work values with trans people

Values are at the heart of social work practice. As well as respecting service users as individuals, social workers must protect the rights and promote the interests of the people for whom they offer services (GSCC, 2010). In their experience of adoption panels, Hartley and Whittle (2003) discuss how trans status is routinely problematised despite evidence to suggest that children brought up in households with a parent who is trans fare as well as other children. Reflecting on how anti-discriminatory principles can be incorporated into their practice with trans people, social workers:

> need to ask themselves if ... they are able to accept different expressions of sex and gender.... Would practitioners regard a child exhibiting male–female tendencies as a 'boy with mental problems' or in contrast 'a girl with physical problems'? Will a 'man with a vagina' or a 'woman with a penis' present problems for professionals in the way they practice and operate? (Hartley and Whittle, 2003:69)

Key questions for social work with trans people

- ➲ How do you ensure that trans people are treated with dignity and respect?
- ➲ How does your placement or agency promote the well-being of trans people?
- ➲ How do your systems monitor gender identity?
- ➲ Have you considered how confidentiality impacts on the lives of trans service users?
- ➲ How do you engage with trans communities locally and are they aware of your services?
- ➲ How does your service welcome trans people?
- ➲ Does the agency display positive images or materials that reflect the lives of trans people?

Further reading

Hines, S. (2007) '(Trans)Forming gender: social change and transgender citizenship', *Sociological Research Online*, 12(1). Available at: http://www.socresonline.org.uk/12/1/hines.html

Kessel, A. (2009) 'Gold medal athlete Caster Semenya told to prove she is a woman', *The Guardian*. Available at: http://www.guardian.co.uk/sport/2009/aug/19/caster-semenya-gender-verification-test

Mitchell, M. and Howarth, C. (2009) *Trans Research Review*. Manchester: Equality and Human Rights Commission.

Mottet, L. and Tanis, J. (2008) *Opening the Door to the Inclusion of Transgender People*. Washington, DC: National Lesbian and Gay Task Force Policy Institute.

Parliamentary Forum on Transsexualism (2005) 'Guidelines for health organisations commissioning treatment services for individuals experiencing gender dysphoria and transsexualism'. Available at: www.pfc.org.uk

Turner, L., Whittle, S. and Combs, R. (2009) 'Transphobic hate crime in the European Union', ILGA-Europe and Press for Change. Available at: http://www.pfc.org.uk (accessed 12 April 2010).

West, P. (2004) *Report into the Medical Needs of Transgender People in Brighton and Hove.* Brighton: Spectrum.

Whittle, S., Turner, L. and Al-Alami, A. (2007) 'Engendered penalties: transgender and transsexual people's experiences of inequality and discrimination', report commissioned by the Equalities Review. Available at: www.pfc.org.uk (accessed 27 April 2007).

Whittle, S., Turner, L., Combs, R. and Rhodes, S. (2008) 'Transgender Eurostudy: legal survey and focus on the transgender experience of health care in EU', International Lesbian and Gay Organisation. Available at: http://www.pfc.org.uk/files/ILGA_report.pdf (accessed 12 April 2010).

Whittle, S. and Turner, L. (2008) *Leading Trans Equality: A Toolkit for Colleges.* Lancaster: Centre for Excellence in Leadership.

Resources for social work with trans people

Bereavement: A Guide for Transsexual, Transgender People and Their Loved Ones., London: Department of Health. Available at: http://services.pfc.org.uk/files/Bereavement.pdf

Trans: a Practical Guide for the NHS, London: Department of Health.

Transgender Experiences: Information and Support, London: Department of Health. Available at: www.dh.gov.uk/en/Publicationsandstatistics/Publications/PublicationsPolicyAndGuidance/DH_097169

An Introduction to Working with Transgender People: Information for Health and Social Care Staff, London: Department of Health. Available at: http://www.dh.gov.uk/en/Publicationsandstatistics/Publications/PublicationsPolicyAndGuidance/DH_074257

'Planning for later life: transgender people', Age Concern. Available at: http://www.ageconcern.org.uk/AgeConcern/Documents/IS30TransgenderJan2007.pdf

World Professional Association for Transgender Health (WPATH), www.wpath.org/

Criminal justice

'Policy for prosecuting cases of homophobic and transphobic crime', Crown Prosecution Service. Available at: http://www.cps.gov.uk/Publications/docs/htc_policy.pdf

'Guidance on prosecuting cases of homophobic and transphobic crime', Crown Prosecution Service. Available at: http://www.cps.gov.uk/Publications/docs/htc_guidance.pdf

'Homophobic and transphobic crime toolkit: good practice and lessons learnt', Crown Prosecution Service. Available at: http://www.cps.gov.uk/publications/prosecution/htc_toolkit.html

Children and young people

Practice scenario

Matthew is a 15-year-old young man who attends a school for children who have emotional and behavioural difficulties. He has been in the care of the local authority since the age of 11 as his parents were drug users and were unable to meet his basic needs. While living with his birth family, he had been socialised to accept the abuse perpetrated against his younger siblings and at times he was an active participant in this. Since being in care, he has experienced 12 placement moves and he currently lives in a small residential home where he receives one-to-one support. The school have engaged in a therapeutic programme with him and he is currently more settled and enjoying both his school and home life. He came out as bisexual to his social worker six months ago but does not want the staff or young people at the residential home, the school or his birth family to know. Recently, he told his social worker that he was seeing a cool guy (aged 21) who he met in the park and he has begun a sexual relationship with him.

Questions

This chapter discusses some of the issues experienced by children and young people who are coming out as lesbian, gay, bisexual or trans. Consider the following questions as you read the chapter to inform the knowledge, skills and values that underpin your social work practice with Matthew:

- What are your learning objectives as a social worker in your work with Matthew?
- Identify the focus of your enquiry.
- What resources and people can support your work with him?
- What are the potential alternative courses of action?

Introduction

Children and young people have been at the centre of two of the most contested pieces of legislation relating to LGBT people. In 1986, a children's book entitled *Jenny lives with Eric and Martin*, which was stocked in the library of the Inner London Education Authority, caused huge media controversy because it was the first to discuss the everyday family life experiences of a child (five-year-old Jenny) and her gay male parents. The ensuing debate led to the introduction of arguably one of the most regressive pieces of legislation, the Local Government Act 1988, which outlawed the promotion of homosexuality in schools and prohibited teaching about the acceptability of homosexuality as a 'pretended' family relationship. During the 1990s, the age of consent was the highest-profile issue in LGBT politics. The legal age for sex between men (sex between women has never been illegal) was reduced from 21 to 18 and then to 16; this equalised the age of consent with that for heterosexual young people.

Policy, guidance and legislation

The Children Act 1989 (and the Children (Scotland) Act 1995) signalled a new direction in children's social policy by promoting children's rights; specifically a child's right to have their feelings and wishes taken into account bearing in mind their age and perceived level of understanding. The Act introduced duties that required local authorities to make due consideration of religion, racial and cultural origin, and linguistic background (section 22 and Schedule 2(11)). Subsequent guidance has recognised that children are not a homogeneous group: their identities, needs and aspirations are shaped by their 'race', class, gender, disability, religion and age. Moreover, a child's sexuality should be acknowledged as a valued part of their identity. The assessment framework for children and their families (DH, 2000a) identifies dimensions of children's developmental needs stating that identity:

> concerns the child's growing sense of self as a separate and valued person. Includes the child's view of self and abilities, self image and self esteem, and having a positive sense of individuality. Race, religion, age, gender, sexuality and disability may all contribute to this. Feelings of belonging and acceptance by family, peer group and wider society, including other cultural groups. (DH, 2000a: 19)

The *Practice Guidance* (DH, 2000b) that accompanies the assessment framework includes sexual identity in its identity model (p 45) and recognises that sexual orientation may form grounds on which children are discriminated against: 'Race, gender, class, disability, age, sexual identity, are all features of group identity which have an outcome for group members in terms of institutional discrimination and disadvantage' (DH, 2000b: 43). However, while the document goes on to discuss how 'race', ethnicity, disability and religion should be taken into account when assessing children's needs, no further mention is made of sexual identity (except in relation to disabled children).

The psychological health of lesbian, gay, bisexual and trans (LGBT) children was included in Standard 9 of the National Service Framework for Children, Young People and Maternity Services 2004 and includes a commitment to provide services on an equal basis:

> Services for children and young people should be provided irrespective of their gender, race, religion, ability, culture or sexuality. This standard emphasises the importance of improving access to CAMHS to ensure greater equity is achieved. (NSF, 2004: 8)

Every Child Matters

Every Child Matters was introduced in 2003 in England and Wales in response to the Laming inquiry into the tragic death of Victoria Climbié. The Green Paper implemented comprehensive reforms in children's services with a preventive agenda that linked child protection to a wider strategy of improving life chances and reducing child poverty. Five outcomes at the heart of this programme of change promised to enable children and young people to fulfil their life potential. These outcomes have relevance for young LGBT people:

1. Be healthy
   - Physically healthy:
     > Body image concerns among young gay and bisexual men may lead to eating disorders (Williamson, 1999).
   - Mentally and emotionally healthy:
     > Mental health problems – risk of suicide and self-harm (see Chapter 6).
     > Resilience and identity formation (see later in this chapter).
   - Sexually healthy:
     > Information about sexual health, sex and relationships guidance.
   - Healthy lifestyles:
     > Drug use (choose not to misuse alcohol, take illegal drugs).
2. Stay safe
   - Safe from maltreatment, neglect, violence and sexual exploitation
   - Safe from bullying and discrimination:
     > Homophobic bullying in school/family violence.
   - Safe from crime and anti-social behaviour in and out of school:
     > Community safety.

- Have security, stability and are cared for:
  - > Eviction from family home for some young people when they come out as LGBT (Cull et al, 2006).
3. Enjoy and achieve
  - Attend and enjoy school
  - Role models/bullying
  - Achieve personal and social development and enjoy recreation
  - Achieve stretching national educational standards
4. Make a positive contribution
  - Develop positive relationships:
    - > Opportunities to meet other LGBT young people.
  - Develop self-confidence and successfully deal with significant life changes and challenges
  - Self-esteem, identity formation:
    - > Inadequate service provision to promote identity formation among young LGBT people (Sherriff and Pope, 2008).
5. Achieve economic well-being
  - Engage in further education, employment or training on leaving school:
    - > Homophobic bullying may have a detrimental impact on a young person's educational achievement and school attendance (Rivers, 2001).
  - Live in decent homes and sustainable communities:
    - > Homelessness (Roche, 2005).

Although the vision underpinning *Every Child Matters* aimed to include every child, it did not explicitly address the needs of lesbian, gay and bisexual children and young people or identify how the outcomes may be understood in relation to them. Young LGBT people's mental and emotional health may be adversely affected if their family rejects them when they come out or if the family environment is one in which negative views are expressed about sexual orientation. At school, young LGBT people's ability to enjoy and achieve may be limited by a curriculum that ignores LGBT people, the lack of positive role models or the absence of a policy to tackle homophobic bullying in schools.

Policy and practice guidance identify sexual orientation as an important aspect of a child's development and make clear that in carrying out their statutory duties, social workers must acknowledge a child's sexual orientation as a valued part of their identity. Unlike practice guidance for other dimensions of a child's identity, in particular, 'race', disability and religion, there are no explicit instructions for social workers in relation to health, education, emotional and behavioural development, family and social relationships or pointers for practice (see also DH, 2000b: 37–53). This means that social workers are sometimes ill-equipped to positively address issues about identity development among young lesbian, gay and bisexual people. Social workers may avoid discussing sexual orientation due to concerns about being considered homophobic, when in fact the circumstances indicate that they should do so as in the case of the Wakefield foster carers (Parrott et al, 2007). But there are everyday situations where social workers do not talk about sexual orientation out of embarrassment or from a belief that it is a personal matter that is irrelevant to social work practice. Many young people may have been taunted for being LGBT and a direct question may not facilitate an open discussion. Young people say that a good social worker will talk to them about their feelings and how they can help, rather than focusing only on problems and their identity (Morrison, 2008). But they also recognise that there are times when social workers may have concerns about how their family or carers, people at school or in their community might react. *Our Journey: Child Protection and LGBT Young People* (Morrison, 2008), a report commissioned by the Scottish government, is based on one of the few studies to investigate the views of young LGBT people about child protection and sought to identify the support and guidance that professionals need to keep children from harm and meet their needs.

Underpinning knowledge

Homophobic bullying

Homophobic bullying takes place 'kind of everywhere': in schools, families, public spaces, on the street, on public transport and in out-of-school activities and sports (Mishna et al, 2009). Although there is increasing acceptance, bullying of LGBT young people is a continuing problem:

> things have come a long way, but I think it's still happening … I don't think I've talked to any … school students who haven't gone through something. The severity differs from person to person, but for sure it still runs rampant in schools. (Mishna et al, 2009: 1602)

The word 'gay', as in 'that's so gay', is in common usage as a form of everyday bullying among young people. The term 'you're so gay' is used against any young person whose behaviour or appearance does not conform to traditional gender norms. Achieving the outcomes of *Every Child Matters* for LGBT young people may be compromised if they are at risk of homophobic bullying (Lukins, 2008). Evidence suggests that they may be at greater risk of bullying and victimisation than other young people (House of Commons

Select Committee, Education and Skills, 2007). A report by Stonewall found that homophobic bullying was commonplace in schools in England and Wales: verbal abuse, cyber-bullying and physical abuse were among the most common (Hunt and Jensen, 2007). There were gender differences in types of bullying: young women were more likely to have been isolated by their peers, while young men were likely to have had their property stolen or vandalised. Half of the young people who took part in *The School Report* (Hunt and Jensen, 2007) said they heard anti-gay remarks on a regular basis. Most young LGBT people had never told anyone they were being bullied: their reasons included the fear that they would not be believed and fear of reprisal (Mishna et al, 2009). Among those who had told someone, most reported that interventions were infrequent and ineffective and that there was no sanction for the bully (Hunt and Jensen, 2007). A study published in the *British Journal of Social Work* suggested that individual-level strategies risk contributing to the problem; by contrast, interventions that draw on eco-mapping may identify the social spaces of vulnerability and domains that might offer support (Mishna et al, 2009). Those who are bullied may suffer from low self-esteem, truant from school, have lower attainment levels and leave education earlier. The long-term effects may include poor mental health, risk of self-harming behaviour and suicide. If the school has implemented a policy to tackle homophobic bullying, LGBT pupils are more likely to feel safe at school, to feel that their school has helped them to solve problems with other pupils and to feel able to 'talk to an adult about being gay' (Hunt and Jensen, 2007: 18).

Developing positive LGBT identities

Adolescence is a key developmental milestone for all young people as they achieve a sense of their own identity, negotiate their place in the world and begin to explore sexual relationships. Their healthy development is promoted by individual characteristics such as high self-esteem and psychological well-being. In addition, their social environment and sense of connectedness to their families, schools and communities are important in fostering resilience and in reducing the likelihood of risky behaviours such as suicidal ideation, substance misuse, unprotected sexual behaviour and eating disorders (Saewyc et al, 2009). Some young LGBT people may have less access to these forms of social capital and this may have implications for their mental health and resilience (Saewyc et al, 2009).

Many young people know they are lesbian, gay or bisexual by the age of 11 or 12 or have feelings of being different. Some do not come out to someone else until they are 15 or 16 and this period has been described as the 'isolation years' (Fish, 2006). Growing up as LGBT, young people have often said that they experienced feelings of difference, confusion or shame and they were fearful of being rejected by family and friends. These problems are exacerbated if an adult dismisses their sexual orientation if they do come out. Some say that adults, including health and social care workers, minimise the issue by suggesting that the young person is too young to know or that it is just a 'passing phase'. Adolescence is the period that is the most crucial for targeting support and information.

Coming out is often seen to be the quintessentially LGBT experience and is linked to better mental health. By coming out, the inconsistency is resolved between one's own perceptions (as gay) with that of others (as heterosexual). Coming out is sometimes described as ripples on a pond beginning with oneself and then to widening circles of people including family, friends, colleagues, neighbours and strangers (Gerstel et al, 1989). A number of models have helped understanding about LGBT identity formation. Cass's (1979) six-stage model of homosexual identity formation is widely cited and shares some parallels with black identity development (Cross, 1991).

Cass's (1979) model of homosexual identity formation

- *Stage 1: Identity confusion* – An awareness that homosexuality is relevant to themselves and their behaviour (behaviours such as kissing; or thoughts, emotions or physiological response).
- *Stage 2: Identity comparison* – The person becomes aware of the differences between their own behaviour and self and of how others view them. There is a sense of not belonging to society at large or to family and peers.
- *Stage 3: Identity tolerance* – There is an increased commitment to recognising oneself as LGBT and to acknowledging social, emotional and sexual needs. This results in heightened alienation and to actively seeking out LGBT communities.
- *Stage 4: Identity acceptance* – LGBT environments increasingly play a part in the person's life and one's identity is accepted by other LGBT people. Passing (that is where people take active steps to conceal their sexual identity) has become a routine strategy for compartmentalising one's sexual orientation.
- *Stage 5: Identity pride* – There is a strong sense of group identity and belonging. There is awareness of the incongruency between one's own self-concept as totally acceptable with society's rejection of this concept.
- *Stage 6: Identity synthesis* – LGBT identity is integrated with all other aspects of self. Rather than *the* identity, being LGBT is seen as merely one aspect.

Cass (1979) acknowledges that the model is a broad guideline rather than a template for all people in all situations. It is useful in that it identifies a developmental process based on the notion that one can accept being LGBT as a positively valued status (which at the time was controversial). In both of these models, coming out is a unidirectional experience (from hiding to openness) and dichotomous: one is either 'in the closet' or 'out and proud'. People in the closet are typically described as leading sad and false lives: the socially isolated, older people and those who have only recently acknowledged an LGBT identity (Fish, 2006). By contrast, Kosovsky Sedgwick (1993) has suggested that coming out is a continual process where the closet encroaches on everyday life and 'the deadly elasticity of heterosexual presumption means that … people find new walls springing up around them' (1993: 46). Instead of describing certain kinds of people, disclosure and non-disclosure may be strategic decisions taken in the light of certain situations. They include active non-disclosure (claiming a heterosexual identity); passive non-disclosure (hiding or avoiding questions about identity); passive disclosure (giving clues about identity); and active disclosure (directly telling a social worker about one's identity). Knowing how disclosure occurs enables professionals to be sensitive to potential clues about sexual orientation.

Gender formations among trans children

Sex is one of the defining characteristics about an individual. The first question posed to a parent about their newborn baby is usually: 'Is it a boy or a girl?' Sex is considered unambiguous and determined at birth by the baby's genitals: being a boy depends upon the possession of a penis and being a girl is determined by the presence of a vagina. Although the genitals are the most significant marker of sex; in most cases, decisions are made about a person's sex without having seen the person naked.

Gender is the term used to describe the cultural significance of sex and refers to the social roles associated with being male or female. When physical characteristics are signalled – for example, by sex-appropriate clothing (blue for boys and pink for girls) – this is a cultural preference.

Traditionally, gender has been clearly demarcated. Masculine characteristics have historically comprised social roles such as being the breadwinner, leadership or capability in mathematics. Commonly ascribed feminine qualities have been deemed to include caring for children, responsibility for the home and proficiency in language. Distinct personality traits are attributed to each gender: males are aggressive, independent and unemotional; females are passive, empathic and emotional. Being a man is not only to have a body with certain physical attributes but to behave in ways that have come to symbolise masculinity. Sex and gender are believed to coincide: the biological ability to bear children is associated with the cultural role and responsibility for bringing up children (Fish, 2010).

Some trans people have described feeling that they are trapped inside the wrong body. Many become aware, sometimes from the age of 10 or younger, that the sense of their own gender (their emotional and psychological traits) does not match their body or physical appearance (Xavier et al, 2007). They have strong and ongoing cross-gender identification and the desire to live and be accepted as a member of the opposite sex.

Coming out to parents and carers

Some people are publicly identified as LGBT in every area of their lives, while others tell no one or very few people. Hiding one's sexual orientation can be a source of stress and anxiety because of concerns about involuntary disclosure or the possibility of rejection by family and friends. When young people come out as LGBT, adults sometimes respond by saying that it is a passing phase. Understanding the process of positive identity formation enables social workers with looked-after children and those in other settings to work with LGBT young people in ways that are likely to be supportive of this process rather than dismissive. In the following extract, the young gay man describes his mother's reaction to his disclosure:

> I came out to my mum … I think the first thing she said, oh I hope you don't move in with any men. I think that was the first thing she actually said. And, if I remember correctly I think she said, I don't mind but I don't want to have to hear about it basically. So she, she, she *accepted* in a sense but just didn't want to, you know, get into any details – she didn't want to know if I was going out with somebody or who I was going out with or what bars I went to – any details you know. (Johnson et al, 2007: 45, emphasis added)

Although he describes his mother's reaction as accepting, her first response is to emphasise what he should not do. Although she says she does not mind that he is gay, she does not want to know anything about his feelings or what he might do. It could be described as a transparent closet where his gayness is visible but the glass walls prevent discussion about his emotions, relationships or where he socialises. While outright rejection is not expressed, the response may be described as tolerating his identity rather than approval. Parents may also feel that if their child comes out as LGBT that it is a negative reflection on their parenting and blame themselves. Moreover, some parents fear social disapproval or consider their child's sexual orientation as their fault. For some young people, the disclosure of their sexual orientation to parents and siblings led to being forced to leave the family home. For others who had yet to come out, the fear of rejection increased their distress and sense of isolation. The process of self-acceptance has been described by a number of models (eg Cass, 1979), but there has not been a corresponding analysis of the ways in which parents and carers respond to the disclosure of LGBT identity and whether they go through a staged process of acceptance.

Mental health and resilience

The experience of conflict with family or peers may mean that young LGBT people are more vulnerable to mental health problems or thoughts of suicide (King et al, 2003; Johnson et al, 2007). Scourfield et al (2008) argue that social workers face the complex task of balancing the need to be alert to heightened risk while avoiding a deficit model which assumes that LGBT young people are necessarily harmed by hostile environments. Developing positive LGBT identities makes particular demands on young people because it requires them to define themselves in contexts where heterosexuality is a privileged identity and being LGBT is stigmatised. One of the distinct issues facing young LGBT people is that, unlike other marginalised groups, they often do not have family or friends who represent LGBT culture:

> [they] live in a world where heterosexuality is the dominant sexual orientation. When heterosexual identities are defined as 'normal' and recognised as the only acceptable sexual orientation, those that identify as 'other' are made invisible, and may be viewed as deviant or unnatural, with the prospect of being targeted for outright violence. Whether or not they experience violence directly, the threat of violence serves to keep many individuals from acknowledging their sexual orientation. (Wexler et al, 2009: 568)

Coming out as LGBT can sometimes be an isolating experience; but being LGBT is not in itself a risk factor for suicide or eating disorders. Rather, it is the response to their coming out that is important. Developing a politicised sense of identity in which a young person is able to reconceptualise their 'personal difficulty as collective struggle' (Wexler et al, 2009: 566) highlights how some young LGBT people in the face of considerable adversity are able to develop resilience and resistance.

Recent research has investigated the strategies used by LGBT young people to promote their own survival. Family connectedness may act as a protective factor alongside safety at school (Eisenberg and Resnick, 2006). Young people develop resilience and self-esteem by resisting discrimination and 'fighting back' when bullied (Scourfield et al, 2008: 332). One of the most common strategies of resilience is finding safe places and safe people to support them in constructing positive LGBT identities. Those young people who were in contact with supportive organisations were enthusiastic about the support they received. But mainstream provision is often inadequate and targeted services lack staff and sustainable funding (Sherriff and Pope, 2008).

Sexual health

The sexual health needs of young people are often talked about within a medical framework that focuses on sexually transmitted infections and unplanned pregnancies. Social workers have a role in providing information and advice to young people to help reduce risky sexual behaviours. But they can also offer support so that sexual health is seen in the context of the whole of a young person's life and includes recognition of their social circumstances and the emotional concerns which impact on their sexual health. This dual role is important because young lesbian and bisexual women are often considered to have no sexual health needs (they are not included in the National Strategy for Sexual Health) because they are considered to be at lower risk for sexually transmitted infections and unplanned pregnancies. There is some suggestion that young LGBT people engage in sexual activity at an earlier age than their heterosexual peers as a way of answering questions about their identity.

The provision of information to young people and the age at which they begin to have sex was contested in the courts by Victoria Gillick in the mid-1980s who argued that her 15-year-old daughter should not have been given contraceptive advice by a health professional without her knowledge. Lord Fraser, in the House of Lords ruling on the case, outlined criteria, commonly known as the Fraser Guidelines, which clarify the circumstances in which advice and information may be given. These were subsequently issued by the Department of Health (DH, 2001a) as guidance for field social workers, residential social workers and foster carers. The guidelines clarify that social workers can actively encourage young people to access sexual health information and services when they are likely to become sexually active.

The 2001 National Strategy for Sexual Health and HIV aimed to tackle the rising rates of sexually transmitted infections, promising better prevention, better services and better sexual health. The strategy recognised that sexual health affects our physical and psychological well-being and acknowledged its importance in some of the most important and lasting relationships in our lives. Inequalities in sexual health mean that the burden of sexual ill-health is borne by women, gay men, teenagers, young adults and black and minority ethnic groups. Globally, social workers have provided essential leadership and support in mobilising community responses to HIV/AIDS. The International Federation of Social Workers issued a social work manifesto to emphasise the relevance of HIV for social work. Many local authorities in the UK offer support through specialist HIV social workers.

Sigma Research has undertaken large-scale sexual health and HIV research among gay men in the UK since 1997, notably the Gay Men's Sex Survey. The most recent study, which included 547 young men, showed the greatest unmet need and knowledge gaps in young gay and bisexual men under the age of 20: they were least likely to have approached services for advice about HIV. The report recommended that prevention services should provide easily accessible, age-appropriate information online about safer sex and HIV (Hickson et al, 2007).

Adoption and LGBT prospective parents

In making decisions about matching a child with a prospective family, adoption panels preferred to place children with traditional two-parent heterosexual families. Considerations about the suitability of LGBT people as potential adopters often assumed that their parenting capacity would be inhibited by their mental health, their relationship quality or stability, and their parenting skills (Ryan et al, 2004; Hicks, 2005). Some adoption agencies assumed that a child's psychosocial development would be negatively affected if their adoptive parents were LGBT. These assumptions included that children brought up by two men (or two women) fail to develop appropriate gender roles and behaviour (girls brought up by lesbians will be tomboyish; boys brought up by gay men will be effeminate). It was also assumed that children brought up in a same-sex relationship would themselves grow up to be gay; furthermore, social workers often believed that children would be bullied on account of their parents' sexual orientation (Fish, 2008). Government circulars prohibited joint adoption by LGBT people; paradoxically, there was no restriction on adoption by LGBT people as individuals. The introduction of the Civil Partnership Act 2004 amended existing adoption legislation: LGBT people are now eligible to apply to jointly adopt children. The 'best interests of the child' form the criteria against which decisions are made about placing a child with a family: social workers should make recommendations to adoption panels based on what is best for the child and not the needs and wishes of potential adopters or the personal opinions of social workers or other child welfare professionals.

Eating disorders

Some studies suggest that young gay and bisexual men may be particularly vulnerable to eating disorders (Austin et al, 2004). Unlike young heterosexual women, to whom they have often been compared, concern about their weight is not the biggest issue. Instead, eating disorders may be linked to aspirations of the ideal gay male body shape, which is both slim and muscular; there is also some evidence which suggests that gay men believe that muscularity offers protection against homophobic hate crime (Kaminski et al, 2005). Although few studies have considered lesbian and bisexual young women and body dissatisfaction, they are unlikely to be immune to eating disorders.

Homelessness

Family intolerance and societal homophobia may contribute to the loss of stable housing or make homelessness more likely for lesbian, gay and bisexual young people (Roche, 2005). *Out on My Own* (Cull et al, 2006), a study conducted among homeless 16–25-year-old LGBT people in Brighton, revealed that some of the causes of homelessness were related to young people's sexual orientation. Some young people were asked to leave the family home by parents who could not accept their sexual orientation or they became runaways and left home before their parents could find out. Others became homeless because they felt isolated in their local community and moved to cities with larger LGBT populations. Homophobia from other tenants in supported housing contributed to further episodes of homelessness (Cull et al, 2006). Two thirds of the young people in the study had been bullied at school and among those who had truanted from school or been excluded, this was linked to educational underachievement. In accessing local authority homelessness services, many LGBT young people said that staff were unhelpful, making it difficult for them to be properly assessed (Cull et al, 2006). The National Youth Homelessness Scheme recommends that local authorities should develop policies that address:

■ the accessibility of homelessness services for LGBT young people, ensuring that the particular needs of these young people are recognised and supported; and
■ preventive measures that recognise parental intolerance and homophobic bullying in schools (CLG and DCSF, 2010).

Guidance for social workers about the provision of accommodation includes consideration of sexual identity when assessing homeless 16- and

17-year-olds (CLG and DCSF, 2010: 20). Student social workers on placement in homelessness agencies or in supported housing need to be aware of the possible causes of homelessness among LGBT young people and alert to the distinctive issues facing them, as in the following example of a young person in a study in Wales: 'They weren't homophobic, they just didn't understand my housing needs – that I did not want to share a room with a man' (gay man commenting on living in a hostel, in Stonewall and Triangle Wales, 2006: 29).

Gold (2005) has produced a good practice guide and the following agencies offer specialist services: Stonewall Housing Association, Albert Kennedy Trust, St Basils and the Outpost Housing Project.

Conclusion

The range of settings of social worker practise with LGBT young people include residential or foster care, child and adolescent mental health services, housing and homelessness projects, and projects specifically targeted to young LGBT people. But there has been a lack of information to support young LGBT people in crisis and few resources to promote the development of a positive identity. This absence was noted by the Scottish Social Work Inspection Agency (SSWIA) in its report *Extraordinary Lives* (SSWIA, 2006), and it acknowledged the importance of finding out more about the needs of looked-after LGBT young people. Since then, the Scottish Institute for Residential Childcare has drawn up practice guidelines outlining some of the common issues in work with young LGBT people (Morrison, 2008). Some young people who took part in the study stated that residential childcare workers sometimes believed that if young people come out as LGBT they pose a threat to others and assume, particularly if the young person is under 16, that there may be child protection concerns. This problem-focused frame of reference meant that:

> Rather than talking about aspects of the young person's life positively they might have conversations which are about challenging the young person's LGBT identity, focusing on worries about mental health or drug or alcohol use, or sexual activity in isolation. (Morrison, 2008: 21)

The guidelines make explicit that young LGBT people are no more likely to be a threat to others than their heterosexual peers. Moreover, in residential care, young people live in close proximity to each other and protecting their privacy is a key concern: some young people will feel very vulnerable in a public care setting if their sexual orientation becomes known. The model draws on a strengths-based approach encompassing four themes:

Vulnerability versus empowerment
- Monitor heterosexist bias.
- Intervene by challenging homophobic remarks.
- Support young people to determine whether to come out and without pressure to do so.

Stigmatisation versus validation
- Support young people to develop resilience to cope with stereotypes.
- Affirm struggles in identity development.
- Reframe difference in gender presentation and behaviour.
- Connect young people with supportive organisations.
- Develop relevant resources.

Acceptance versus rejection
- Acknowledge sexual orientation in an appropriate matter-of-fact way.
- Communicate acceptance and demonstrate that LGBT identities are highly valued.
- Celebrate difference and diversity.
- Maintain a position of active engagement: young people's developmental experiences are individual.

Policies and practice in residential care
- Consider recording practices and care planning
- Anti-homophobic bullying policy
- If there are no child protection concerns, the young person's choice about what is recorded should be paramount (adapted from Sutherland, 2009: 3).

Exercise

Drawing on issues explored in this chapter, use Table 5.1 to highlight key issues to promote the welfare of LGBT children and young people. Identify relevant issues and resources to underpin your knowledge, values and skills.

Table 5.1: Using the assessment framework to safeguard and promote the welfare of LGBT young people

Child or young person's developmental needs	Summary of issues identified	Identifying relevant resources
Health	Sexual health Mental health Emotional well-being	For example, www.pacehealth.org.uk
Education	Anti-homophobic bullying policy/practice Role models LGBT young people represented in school curriculum Positive images of LGBT young people	For example, Schools Out, www.schools-out.org.uk
Identity	Opportunities to develop a positive identity through meeting others Gaining support from family and friends Positive reinforcement	For example, the Stonewall (no date) guide on supporting LGBT young people
Family and social relationships	How can the family provide support? Opportunities to meet other LGBT young people	For example, the Stonewall report *Different families*, www.stonewall.org.uk/at_home/parenting/default.asp
Social presentation	How do they feel about presenting themselves to the world? Do they feel a pressure to 'look gay' or to pass as heterosexual or neither of these? Gender presentation and behaviour	For example, http://transforum.org.uk/
Emotional and behavioural development	Are they supported to explore their feelings about themselves? Is there an environment where they can deal with stigma and discrimination? Are they supported to develop appropriate relationships with others?	For example, youth groups/projects, www.allsortsyouth.org.uk Lesbian and Gay Foundation Manchester, www.manchesterconcord.org.uk

Child or young person's developmental needs	Summary of issues identified	Identifying relevant resources
Self-care skills	Able to deal with negative reactions	*It Gets Better* – YouTube video – see Resources section below
Family and environmental factors	How supportive is the environment of the town/city in which they live?	For example, International Day against Homophobia (IDAHO)
Community resources	What resources are available locally? Access to groups for LGBT young people	Stonewall database What's in my area?
Heritage	LGBT history	LGBT history month, films, books, Pride events

Source: Adapted from DH (2000a).

Further reading

Cross, W.E. (1991) *Shades of Black: Diversity in African-American Identity*, Philadelphia: Temple University Press.

Guasp, A. (2010) *Different Families: The Experiences of Children with Lesbian and Gay Parents*, London: Stonewall.

Hunt, R. and Jensen, J. (2007) *The School Report: The Experiences of Young Gay People in Britain's Schools*, London: Stonewall.

Lukins, M. (2008) 'If every child matters what about us? Young people's experiences of homophobic bullying in Southampton schools', unpublished dissertation, Southampton.

Morrison, C. (2008) 'Our journey: child protection and LGBT young people', LGBT Youth Scotland. Available at: http://www.LGBTyouth.org.uk/portalbase/pages/download.aspx?locationId=16fd28e9-294b-4153-87d6-d8bf571068ad (accessed 27 July 2010).

National Lesbian and Gay Task Force (no date) 'GLBT parents and their children'. Available at: http://www.thetaskforce.org/downloads/reports/reports/LGBTParentsChildren.pdf (accessed 23 July 2010).

Ryan, C. (2009) 'Helping families support their lesbian, gay, bisexual, and transgender (LGBT) children'. Available at: http://nccc.georgetown.edu/documents/LGBT_Brief.pdf (15 December 2010).

SSWIA (Scottish Social Work Inspection Agency) (2006) *Extraordinary Lives: Creating a Positive Future for Looked after Children in Scotland*, Edinburgh: Scottish Social Work Inspection Agency.

Stonewall (no date) 'Supporting lesbian, gay and bisexual young people'. Available at: http://www.stonewall.org.uk/at_school/education_resources/4562.asp (23 July 2010).

Sutherland, M. (2009) *In Residence: Practice Applications for Residential Childcare*, Edinburgh: Scottish Institute for Residential Childcare.

Resources

YouTube clips:'It gets better', www.youtube.com/watch?v=7IcVyvg2Qlo: in response to the suicide of a gay teenager in September 2010, a journalist set up an online video project – 'It gets better' – to offer messages of support to young people who are bullied because they are LGBT. A similar project was launched by Stonewall in the UK. Available at: http://www.stonewall.org.uk/what_you_can_do/campaigning_opportunities/it_gets_better_today/4844.asp

Older people

Practice scenario

Walter is a gay man in his early eighties who lives in a village in a rural area. He is currently in hospital following a fall in his garden where he spends much of his time. The hospital doctors want to discharge him and he has been receiving physiotherapy so he can now walk with a walking aid. Although Walter has lived in his current home since his retirement 15 years ago, he is a private person and is known by his neighbours to keep himself to himself. He is not 'out' to them and he is careful not to reveal personal details of his life. His friends, who are also older gay men, live in a city 20 miles away and he has tended to travel to see them. In the assessment of his care needs, Walter says that he does not want to go into a residential care home but he is worried about coping alone.

Questions
This chapter discusses some of the issues experienced by older LGBT people. Consider the following questions as you read the chapter to inform your assessment of Walter's needs:

- What are your learning objectives in your work with Walter?
- Identify the focus of your enquiry.
- What resources and people can support your work with him?
- What are the potential alternative courses of action?
- What knowledge, skills and values underpin social work practice with Walter?

Introduction

The 'baby boom' generation, people born in the post–war period (1945–64), represent a significant demographic group currently approaching retirement. It is estimated that in the next 25 years, older people in the population will outnumber those under 16 for the first time. Baby boomers were born at the time the modern welfare state came into being: better living and working conditions and universal health care have contributed to increased longevity. During the 1930s, men could expect to live until the age of 53 and women until age 59. Current life expectancy is age 76 and 80 for men and women, respectively. Although the welfare state has offered social protection for people as they grow older, its founding principles were constituted around the notion of the heterosexual, nuclear family. These ideologies have shaped the provision of social care and contributed to inequalities for LGBT communities (Concannon, 2007).

Social work services are demarcated at the state retirement age: those who are aged 65 and over come under the remit of older people's services. The focus on chronological age has a tendency to homogenise older people: not only will people's needs differ widely depending on whether they are 65 or 85, but among those who are 65, there will be considerable difference in levels of mobility and independence. Although ageism is prohibited by legislation, stereotyping and prejudicial attitudes persist, including assumptions that older people are a burden on the state, unable to make their own decisions, lonely and asexual.

Underpinning knowledge

Perceptions of ageing in LGBT communities

The meanings attached to ageing shape how one sees oneself and how one is perceived by others. Early research offered a negative portrayal of ageing in which older gay men, in particular, were depicted as lonely, isolated and tragic (Pugh, 2005). One theory suggested the concept of accelerated ageing where gay men were found to view themselves as old at a younger age than heterosexual men (Schope, 2005). Studies have also examined whether lesbians and gay men have more negative perceptions of ageing and found significant differences along gender lines. Gay men are more likely than lesbians to say that being older is considered negatively in LGBT communities. They believed that one becomes old at an earlier age (38 years) than did lesbians (48 years) and they were much less likely to consider a relationship with an older person. Perceptions of ageing are said to be more negative among gay men because they place more importance on other people's evaluations of their physical attractiveness (Schope, 2005). (Despite these differences, however, the study did find that almost 40% of gay men viewed their own growing older in positive terms.) Other explanations suggest that the dominance of the commercial gay scene and its youth-oriented culture serves to exclude older gay men from taking part or they choose to be less involved as they grow older (Heaphy et al, 2003).

Impact of homophobia and heterosexism

Older LGBT people constitute a generation who have lived through a time when homosexuality was illegal, labelled a psychiatric disorder or considered sinful (Fish, 2006). Consequently, many older LGBT people have spent their lives hiding their sexual orientation even from close family members:

> Hiding from wider society the actual nature of one's sexual identity and sexual relationships, concealing the depth of one's emotional partnerships to particular people or gender groups, masking one's participation in the activities associated with a sexual minority community, and obscuring the true nature of one's identity and feelings in the mainstream world of family, school, and work, all have lifelong and serious consequences. (Barker et al, cited in SAGE, 2010: 5)

The climate of the post-war period was hostile towards LGBT people. In one incident, which typifies social attitudes, the celebrated actor, John Gielgud, was entrapped by an undercover policeman in a public toilet in the early 1950s. Many others were not only fined but also imprisoned for being gay. The resulting social humiliation meant that many LGBT people were subject to extortion and threats. The incident contributed to the establishment of the Wolfenden Committee whose work culminated in the decriminalisation of homosexuality by the Sexual Offences Act 1967. Habits of being private and careful about coming out to others have had enduring effects on the personal lives of older LGBT people. Some maintained distant relationships with their families of origin to reduce the likelihood of disclosure; while others, who did come out, were disowned by their family (Quam et al, 2010). Non-disclosure has meant that LGBT people have been invisible in public services making it difficult for social workers and other professionals to undertake assessments of their health and social care needs. Their reasons for not coming out include the fear of discrimination or the expectation of poor treatment if their identity was known: 'I feel I'd be better off home and alone than feeling humiliated by other residents or even worse, the people I'd depend on for my health care, my medicine' (Stein et al, 2010: 429).

Other participants in the study talked about negative past experiences of visiting friends or partners in nursing homes and hoped to avoid being housed in a mainstream long-term care setting. A study conducted by the US Administration on Aging found that LGBT people were five times less likely than heterosexual people to access public services, including day services for older people and housing assistance (cited in Stein et al, 2010). Older LGBT people identified discrimination as one of their greatest concerns about ageing (Metlife, 2006); three quarters of those taking part in a survey conducted by Age Concern were concerned about moving into sheltered accommodation or a residential home because of expectations of discrimination (Phillips and Knocker, 2010).

Sexuality and older people

Older people in general are believed to be asexual and no longer interested in sexual activity. Being LGBT is seen to be something that one *does* rather than something one *is*, that is, being LGBT is associated with sexual behaviour rather than an identity that persists whether or not one engages in sexual activity. If a heterosexual man or woman no longer engaged in sex, they may describe themselves as celibate; it is unlikely they would say they were no longer heterosexual. Being LGBT is widely seen as a sexualised identity; the stereotype that older people are asexual leads some providers to assume that older people are no longer LGBT.

Social connectedness and loneliness in LGBT communities

Loneliness is more common among people who do not have a partner or children and among those with a smaller social circle. Unlike other marginalised groups, such as black and minority ethnic (BME) and refugee communities, where the Church may provide a focal role in community-building, there have been few spaces for LGBT people to socialise and develop their networks. The commercial scene of pubs and clubs has often provided meeting places for LGBT people, but the focus on a youth–oriented culture means that these venues offer a less comfortable environment in which to meet others for LGBT older people. HIV/AIDS has also had a disproportionate impact on this generation: many gay and bisexual men have lost a partner while others in the LGBT community have lost friends to the disease. The combination of these issues has led to assumptions about lower levels of social capital among LGBT older people. Research conducted in the Netherlands found that LGBT older people were lonelier and less socially embedded than heterosexual older people; they had less intensive contact with their family; were more likely to be childless; and were less frequent churchgoers (Fokkema and Kuyper, 2009). In comparison to their heterosexual counterparts, they were less likely to have a partner and were more likely to live alone (Stein et al, 2010). A common living arrangement among those with a partner was each maintaining a separate home; the researchers conceptualised this as a Living Apart Together (LAT) relationship (Fokkema and Kuyper, 2009). This Dutch study is one of the first to consider whether LGBT older people are lonelier than their heterosexual peers because of fewer social networks. It revealed that they were significantly more lonely and this difference was greater among men (19% of gay men and 14% of lesbians were seriously lonely, while the equivalent scores for heterosexual older people were 2% of men and 5% of women) (Fokkema and Kuyper, 2009). The researchers found, however, that increased loneliness was only partly explained by weaker social connectedness. They argued that the quality of social relationships was significant: older LGBT people felt lonelier because they 'miss depth, intimacy, recognition and understanding in their existing relationships' (Fokkema and Kuyper, 2009: 274). The implications suggest that social workers should seek to validate, rather than ignore, older LGBT people's personal networks.

Families of choice

Families of origin may have offered little support or been distant from their LGBT relatives. In the face of disapproval or estrangement, LGBT people have forged networks of partners, former partners, friends and supportive family members as their 'families of choice' (Heaphy et al, 2003: 4). They have constructed egalitarian personal networks and reciprocal relationships that are supportive for them as they approach older age (Heaphy, 2009). Older LGBT people may not have close relatives living nearby to call on for help, as one woman said: 'We need each other in a way that heterosexuals don't. We've led a life of nobody being there' (SAGE, 2010).

An important difference is that among heterosexual older people, caregivers are likely to be intergenerational: sons or daughters are likely to be called upon as providers of care. By contrast, families of choice for older LGBT people are likely to be a similar age and may not be able to provide long-term care as they may experience their own health problems. It may be more difficult for friends to provide the intimate and personal care that may be expected from families of origin:

> Close kin, spouses, or children especially feel a responsibility to provide care to family members, out of a sense of love or respect, a feeling of moral obligation, a long history of association, and gratitude for past favors and mutual aid. Kin – particularly close kin – are supposed to provide help for as long as necessary, often without tangible or immediate rewards, and to be willing to take on emotional and instrumental care including, if need be, intimate or personal care such as bathing or toileting. When based on feelings of moral obligation and responsibility, care [from biological family members] is expected to endure as long as necessary, for years even,

until the kin's capacity to provide technically competent care is far exceeded. (Barker et al, cited in SAGE, 2010: 7)

Although there is a growing body of work that identifies friends as equivalent to family, relatively little is known about the nature of coupled relationships in LGBT communities. Studies among younger LGBT people (studies have not been conducted among trans communities) have found that they are characterised by an equitable division of household labour where couples see themselves as equals in the sharing of roles (eg Dunne, 1997). Quam et al (2010) suggest that social workers may usefully explore the communication styles and conflict resolution methods of older same-sex couples in problem-solving and decision-making.

Residential care and housing choices for older LGBT people

The Department for Communities and Local Government (DCLG) commissioned research as part of the New Ambitions for Old Age Programme. It sought to inform the development of a housing strategy in an ageing society by eliciting the views of neglected communities including disabled people, BME communities and LGBT older people. Most were determined to live in their current home for as long as possible. Across the groups, the decision to move into supported or residential accommodation was influenced by five factors:

- attachment to current home;
- complexity of family/caring relationships;
- neighbours and neighbourhood;
- access to services and amenities; and
- health and well-being (see Croucher, 2008: 7).

The attitudes of neighbours and the wider neighbourhood are of particular importance in shaping the decisions about future accommodation choices for older LGBT people. A study conducted throughout Scotland found that harassment was a problem for a significant minority of older LGBT people and a number had to move home as a consequence (Stonewall Scotland, 2005).

The prospect of living in a residential care home is a concern for many older people as it signals a loss of independence and a move away from a family home that may be associated with treasured memories. These issues may be heightened for older LGBT people who may fear living in close proximity with others who disapprove of them; some older LGBT people may feel obliged to go back into the closet (Croucher, 2008). There is an assumption that secrecy is the only option facing an older person who moves into a residential care home:

> You've always got to watch what you say, so that people who go into homes have to go into the closet and self-censoring themselves, you've got to ... y'know the very tiring mode of censoring yourself, keeping the conversation neutral ... no, I may be being pessimistic, but I think it is back to the closet. (Gay and Grey in Dorset, 2006: 69)

One older person talked about the lack of recognition for his relationship and lack of involvement in decisions affecting his partner's care:

> The staff in the home very rarely gave us any time alone together and on one occasion Arthur was taken seriously ill and was transferred to hospital without them notifying me. The man I love could have died and I wouldn't have been there or even known. (Ian, in Knocker, 2006: 3)

By contrast, an older lesbian found that the approach taken by a member of staff made a difference to her feelings of safety and willingness to come out:

> It was such a relief when the manager of the extra care scheme where I was living encouraged me to open up about my lesbian identity. She didn't push me but she gave me plenty of messages that she didn't have a problem. It immediately helped me to feel that I was accepted for the whole of me, and more important that I felt safe in my own home. (Beatrice, in Knocker, 2006: 3)

These contrasting experiences can have a considerable impact on the quality of life of older LGBT people. There are mixed preferences about whether dedicated housing provision would best meet the needs of older LGBT people. The overwhelming majority of people who took part in a study undertaken by Polari, an organisation for LGBT older people in London, suggested that targeted provision would enable people to maintain existing friendship networks and develop new ones as they grow older (Hubbard and Rossington, 2001). A subsequent study found that 77% wanted provision that was lesbian- and gay-friendly, while a third thought care should be offered by gay providers (Heaphy et al, 2003).

Shared experiences could provide opportunities for oral history work and offer a supportive environment for LGBT people as they age: 'The idea of specific housing and/or sheltered accommodation for elderly gay men and women is a wonderful one. The resulting comfort, support and security would be priceless' (Mike, Wales, in Hubbard and Rossington, 2001: 54).

Others felt that specific accommodation could create 'ghettoes' and become a potential target for homophobic abuse. They also felt that a more integrated approach would widen the housing options and ensure that mainstream providers offer appropriate accommodation. It may be that dedicated provision is no longer the preferred housing option because of efforts to improve residential care for older LGBT people.

Policy and practice issues

Assessment of need

In the UK, a resources pack for residential care managers outlined the requirements for meeting the National Minimum Standards (Care Standards) Act 2000 for assessment and care planning. When new older residents are admitted to a care home, the assessment should consider the person's 'social interests, hobbies, religious and cultural needs' and 'carer and family involvement and other social contacts/relationships' (DH, 2003: 3–4). The NHS and Community Care Act 1990 gives the legal mandate for assessment; current practice prioritises physiological and safety needs (such as installing a handrail on stairs or steps) and is less likely to consider needs for self-esteem, belonging and self-actualisation (Pugh, 2005).

Personalisation and individual budgets

The personalisation agenda has been a key strategy in the reform of social care for over a decade since its introduction. The Community Care (Direct Payments) Act 1996 introduced a new model of service delivery by allowing social services departments to make payments directly to the service user so that they can purchase the services they need. The *Modernising Social Services* White Paper (DH, 1998) signalled the extension of the 'third way' approach to social care by shifting the emphasis from the service provider to promoting the independence of service users. Subsequent policy initiatives, such as *Partnerships for Older People* (DH, 2005), aimed to extend choice and control to older people as they were one of the user groups who were not accessing services through direct payments. Personalisation as an approach can empower service users by enabling them to find appropriate solutions and become actively engaged in choosing and shaping the services they receive. It recognises that a one-size-fits-all approach to service provision does not address the needs of people from diverse communities. In Scotland, three key areas are highlighted for change:

1. *Personalisation as prevention* – building the capacity of individuals and communities to manage their own lives with appropriate and proportionate intervention at the right time. The focus is on: preventative services, self-management, enablement and rehabilitative services.
2. *Personalisation for service users with complex needs* – helping people to find the right support solutions for them and to be active participants in the development and delivery of services. Encourage people to come up with their ideas and put effort into devising solutions that suit them in their particular circumstances drawing on their own strengths, family or community capacity. This does not mean that people are not supported and left without guidance or that risks are not addressed, but that solutions are developed in partnership with professionals.
3. *Personalisation as choice* – sometimes people just want to have efficient, reliable 'off-the-shelf' services that respond to their needs when they have them. Give people access to a choice of services and enable them to speak up for what they want. Views of people who use these services are listened to and issues are acted upon (see Scottish Government, 2009).

But the introduction of direct payments to tailor services to the needs of individuals has not been without controversy. Concern was expressed about the relatively low take-up of direct payments, particularly among older people. A programme of individual budgets was piloted to embed the principles of personalisation in social work practice and because it was assumed that social workers were reluctant to promote direct payments. Individual budgets differ from previous arrangements in a number of ways, they offer (Glendinning et al, 2008: 4):

- a greater role for self-assessment;
- greater opportunities for self-definition of needs and desired outcomes;
- increased opportunities for users to determine for themselves how they want those outcomes to be achieved.

Direct payments and individual budgets transfer the responsibility for commissioning services or employing a care worker from social workers to the service user. An evaluation of individual budgets found different patterns of accessing social services among older people than other service user groups (eg people with mental health problems or people with disabilities):

> Older people often approach services at a time of crisis when they feel vulnerable or unwell and find decision-making difficult. The evaluation indicates that a potentially substantial proportion of older people may experience taking responsibility for their own

support as a burden rather than as leading to improved control. (Glendinning et al, 2008: 238)

Some have argued that direct payments can transform the lives of older LGBT service users: promoting their independence and empowering them to make decisions about the care they receive. One gay man explained that control of his own budget meant that he felt safer that the person providing intimate care was someone of his choosing:

> I would have been imprisoned with a care agency. Can't stress that too strongly. I live at home supported by people I recruit who I am very clear with who I am. They don't change every week.... Life has been a thousand times better on direct payments even with its challenges. (CSCI, 2008: 16)

The success of direct payments or individual budgets is dependent upon the availability of relevant and accessible services and of a pool of care workers who are appropriately trained. One carer with experience of looking after two terminally ill gay partners and of running a support group for the Alzheimer's Society suggested that there may be difficulties in identifying gay-friendly care workers (Gulland, 2009). The transfer of budgets from local authorities to individual service users may also have implications for safeguarding adults. Individual budgets will replace existing provision rather than coexist alongside it. The protocols and systems for ensuring that vulnerable adults are protected from harm are located within local authorities; there are questions about where the responsibility will lie for investigating abuse once funding is transferred.

End-of-life care

The Coalition government has stated its commitment to personalisation in the *Equity and Excellence: Liberating the NHS* White Paper (HMG, 2010), extending its provisions to include end-of-life care (EOLC): 'How people die remains in the memory of those who live on' (DH, 2008b: 1). At the start of the 20th century, most people died in their own homes of an acute infection. One hundred years later, people are more likely to die in a health or social care setting, with four out of five deaths taking place in an NHS hospital, a care home or a hospice following a period of chronic illness (DH, 2008b). These changes mean that it is more likely that social workers in a range of settings including older people's teams, hospitals and in palliative care, alongside residential care managers and care workers, will have some involvement with the family and support networks of the person approaching the end of life. The care provided at the end of life has been a neglected area within the NHS and social services and the quality of that care has been variable. The *End of Life Care Strategy* (DH, 2008b) was introduced to address service variations and to bring about a step change for everyone approaching the end of life. Unlike other policies for older people, the EOLC strategy explicitly includes sexual orientation as a characteristic that must be taken account of in end-of-life care:

> This should be irrespective of age, gender, ethnicity, religious belief, disability, sexual orientation, diagnosis or socioeconomic status. High quality care should be available wherever the person may be: at home, in a care home, in hospital, in a hospice or elsewhere. (DH, 2008b: 10)

End-of-life care has recently emerged as a field of study in recognition that many people are daunted by the prospect of planning for their own death and do not make their preferences known. Many social workers and other professionals have had little training in offering support for service users who are close to death or dying and feel ill-equipped to initiate discussions or to include their wishes in care planning (DH, 2008b). End-of-life care can influence the ways in which friends and family cope with bereavement. For LGBT people, these issues may be compounded by a lack of recognition of their support networks and discrimination in their access to services. *Equity and Excellence: Liberating the NHS 2010* (DH, 2010a) signals a move to support people in their preferences about how to have a good death and identifies the importance of working alongside hospices and other providers to ensure that people have the necessary support. Although people will have different ideas about what a good death might look like, the *End of Life Care Strategy* (DH, 2008b) identifies three aspects of care that contribute towards the best possible care in the final days of life:

- Being treated as an individual, with dignity and respect.
- Being in familiar surroundings.
- Being in the company of close family or friends.

Apart from pain, which is not considered here, these aspects may be experienced differently by LGBT people approaching the end of life. Barbara, a participant in a study of breast cancer (Fish, 2010), talks about an occasion where the health professional did not treat her as an individual and had no concept that the questions asked needed to reflect the reality of her life. Instead, the intake form asked questions on the presumption of her heterosexuality, making it unlikely that she would disclose her sexual orientation and receive holistic healthcare. When she was recovering in hospital a group of friends came to visit her and it was at this point that her sexual orientation became evident to the nurses and other patients on the ward:

> At visiting time I'd have quite a large group of people around my bed and they'd be like men and women and we'd be laughing and joking, not really raucous but … I've got a gallows kind of humour. Where other people would be sitting quite quietly I'm not like that. One woman particularly who … was quite friendly with me until she saw the people that came in to see me, who to me are obviously gay people, men and women. And her husband was quite hostile and made comments under his breath and closed the curtain. It didn't bother me particularly but it did feel a little bit hostile. (Barbara, interview 18, in Fish, 2010)

'Next of kin'

The patient's family is often expected to provide care at the end of life and such cultural expectations may have their use in hospital settings in the notion of 'next of kin'. People who are 'kin' (who are usually blood relatives or the patient's spouse) have taken precedence over others in their visiting rights and in making decisions about treatment and care. Many people in same-sex relationships are concerned that health care workers may refuse them visiting rights or access to information about diagnosis, treatment or care. This information is reserved for the patient's 'next of kin'. In most circumstances, there is no legal basis for this; the term relates to the disposal of property to blood relatives when someone dies without having made a will (RCN, 2005). The Civil Partnership Act 2004 conferred legal recognition to same-sex couples who have registered their partnership, but many LGBT people who are not legally partnered may believe that the term only relates to those who are civil partnered. Asking for a person's next of kin may cause confusion and may not elicit the relevant information.

The lack of validation of same-sex relationships has sometimes meant that an estranged son or daughter who has not been supportive of the parent's same-sex relationship have stepped in and taken over the decision-making at the end of life (Almack et al, 2010). One well-known 'real-life' experience involved an older lesbian couple, Carrie and Anne, who had lived together for over 40 years and were admitted to different nursing homes by distant family members who refused to allow Anne to visit her partner in a nursing home following a stroke. It was only after a social worker had recognised the nature of their relationship that the two women were placed in the same home together three days before Carrie's death. A recent experience was described in an end-of-life study of LGBT people, where Jeremy had no say in his partner's funeral arrangements because his partner, David, had not wanted his family to know that he was gay (Almack et al, 2010). Instead of his status of partner being recognised by David's family, they viewed him only as a friend and excluded him from the funeral arrangements. This lack of acknowledgement has been described as 'disenfranchised grief' (Smolinski, 2006: 56). In this example, the relationship has not been accepted or validated by the family and the bereaved partner's loss is not recognised. The surviving partner may not be able to access other forms of social support where they can express their grief and have their loss acknowledged, as articulated by a research participant in a UK study:

> The problems of losing a (lesbian) partner, after 30 years in my case, are that you have no time to grieve, not being married ... I had no rights ... you're not treated like a couple ... it was horrendous ... I mean 30 years and what had I got to show for it.... The love and the care and the loyalty that we'd shared ... nobody knew about it. (Gay and Grey in Dorset, 2006: 65)

Elaine had a contrasting experience after her partner, Mary, died following a long illness where she had been cared for in a local hospice. Although Elaine had not come out to staff at the hospice, she was acknowledged by them as Mary's partner and offered services to support her in her bereavement (Fish, 2010):

> In the last two years of Mary's life, she went to two of the hospices in the area and I went with her.... And while I was sitting there they asked me what I would like as well and I said, oh it's not me, I'm not the one who has cancer. And they said, it's fine, we also offer services to partners. *I hadn't said a thing.* And so for about eighteen months, you know, I used to go and have aromatherapy, it was really lovely actually, massage and, you know. (Elaine, interview 9, in Fish, 2010, emphasis added)

She valued not having to explain herself ("I hadn't said a thing") and the implicit recognition of her relationship with Mary.

Older LGBT people and dementia

Roger Newman established the LGBT carers' network for the Alzheimer's Society following his partner's diagnosis with pre-senile dementia at the age of 56. Newman describes the necessary dismantling of the protective walls they had constructed around their lives to make themselves anonymous:

> But should the time come when we are suffering from a life-threatening disease, have a requirement of long-term healthcare, have the need to get help from social services, and possibly require residential care, then all those carefully constructed defences are immediately at risk. In short, a new and threatening world suddenly arises for the 60-year-old gay carer at the hospital, the doctor's surgery, or on the phone to a social worker. (Newman, 2005: 266)

Newman struggled to have his relationship acknowledged and professionals often assumed that an HIV test was needed because of stereotyped assumptions about HIV/AIDS among gay men. Gay men whose partners have Alzheimer's report difficulties in getting recognition from service providers that they are the most appropriate person to make decisions about their partners' affairs even when they have power of attorney.

Work with older LGBT people in the voluntary social care sector

Age Concern has worked to raise awareness of the needs of older LGBT people across the statutory and voluntary sectors in social work and social care. Its Opening Doors programme, established in 2001, is the largest funded project working with older LGBT people in the UK. Through Opening Doors, a range of services are offered to older LGBT people in London, including work to combat social isolation and befriending services, community safety events in conjunction with the Metropolitan Police, LGBT history events, advice and information sessions, and a range of social activities. Age Concern have developed training materials, resources and information packs relating to partnership rights, making a will, 'next of kin' and tenancy (Phillips and Knocker, 2010).

Conclusion: working towards good practice with older LGBT people

The need for culturally competent services was underlined by a survey conducted by the Commission for Social Care Inspection (CSCI) which found that although 94% of services reported that they carried out equality and diversity work including staff training, only 9% of providers gave any examples of equality work they have carried out in relation to sexual orientation. This compares to 37% who gave an example relating to race equality and 33% who gave an example relating to disability equality (CSCI, 2008). Services need to proactively demonstrate that their services are inclusive otherwise older LGBT people will assume the worst.

Knocker (2006) identifies good practice in making care homes welcoming and accessible before admission alongside developing a supportive organisational ethos where LGBT issues are raised at staff recruitment, induction and training. Few care workers had received training on how to diffuse and counter hostility from other residents or their families (SAGE, 2010). Only one third of older LGBT people believed health professionals to be positive towards them and fewer considered that professionals were knowledgeable about their concerns (Heaphy et al, 2003). Residential care homes have been reluctant and sometimes hostile to the possibility of an older same-sex couple occupying a shared room and double bed (Fish, 2006). A recent landmark case, which found that a Cornish hotel had discriminated against a gay couple in a civil partnership by refusing them a double bed, may have implications for older same-sex couples and lead to a change in practice and attitudes (Bowcott, 2011).

Key questions for social work with older people

➲ How do you ensure that older LGBT people are treated with dignity and respect?

➲ How do you promote the well-being of older LGBT people?

➲ How do you show value for the positive contribution made by older LGBT people in service provision and in society more generally?

➲ Have you considered how confidentiality impacts on the lives of LGBT service users?

➲ How do you engage with LGBT communities locally and are they aware of your services?

➲ How does your service welcome older LGBT people?

➲ Does the agency display positive images or materials that reflect the lives of LGBT people?

Further reading

DH (Department of Health) (2008) *End of Life Care Strategy: Promoting High Quality Care for All Adults at the End of Life*, London: Department of Health.

Gay and Grey in Dorset (2006) *Lifting the Lid on Sexuality and Ageing*, Bournemouth: Help and Care.

Heaphy, B., Yip, A. and Thompson, D. (2003) *Lesbian, Gay and Bisexual Lives over 50: A Report on the Project 'The Social and Policy Implications of Non-Heterosexual Ageing'*, Nottingham: York House Publications.

Hubbard, R. and Rossington, J. (2001) *As We Grow Older: A Study of the Housing and Support Needs of Older Lesbians and Gay Men*, Polari Housing Association.

Knocker, S. (2006) *The Whole of Me: Meeting the Needs of Older Lesbians, Gay Men and Bisexuals Living in Care Homes and Extra Care Housing*, London: Age Concern.

MetLife (2006) *Out and Aging: The MetLife Study of Lesbian and Gay Baby Boomers*, Westport, CT: MetLife Mature Market Institute.

Musingarimi, P. *(2008) Older Gay, Lesbian and Bisexual People in the UK: A Policy Brief*, London: International Longevity Centre – UK (ILCUK).

SAGE (Services and Advocacy for Gay, Lesbian, Bisexual and Transgender Elders) (2010) *Improving the Lives of LGBT Older Adults*, New York: SAGE.

Smith, A. and Calvert, J. (2001) *Opening Doors: Working with Older Lesbians and Gay Men*, London: Age Concern England.

Stonewall Scotland (2005) *Housing and Support Needs of Older Lesbian, Gay, Bisexual and Transgender (LGBT) People in Scotland*, Edinburgh: Communities Scotland.

Mental health

Practice scenario

Amiyah is a 17-year-old South Asian young woman who is questioning her identity. She was taken into the care of the local authority when she was eight because of sexual abuse in her family. She has bipolar disorder and has started cutting after a period of two years during which time she had stopped self-harming; she says it makes her feel in control of her life and allows her to release her feelings. In discussion with her residential social worker, she says that her abuse has made her lesbian. Until recently, Amiyah was having a relationship with 19-year-old Tonya, but they split up two months ago. Amiyah enjoyed meeting new people (who were mainly Tonya's friends), attending Birmingham Pride and they had planned to go on holiday together. Amiyah had planned to go to university but there is a question about whether her grades will be good enough.

Discussion

A social worker involved in Amiyah's care would be aware that some mental health and other professionals sometimes explain lesbian identity as a response to childhood sexual abuse (Johnson et al, 2007). It may be that she has internalised feelings of low self-worth after hearing such views from workers or it may be that she fears rejection by those around her and shame about her identity and that this is a way of minimising comments from other people. Such negative assumptions might affect her ability to develop self-esteem and a positive identity.

Amiyah may not have the support of her family, although this cannot be assumed. Being brought up in care may mean she lacks positive role models and a supportive network of friends.

Childhood sexual abuse

In the practice scenario, Amiyah believes that sexual abuse in her childhood led to her being lesbian as a young woman. Some studies have found higher rates of sexual abuse in lesbians in comparison to heterosexual women (Hughes et al, 2001). If a woman believes that her identity was formed as a result of sexual abuse, her feelings of shame and internalised homophobia may be intensified. It may be that she accounts for her lesbianism in this way because this means that her identity is neither chosen nor something she was born with, but rather a consequence of her life experiences. It may be a way of deflecting blame for being lesbian. Research conducted in Brighton suggests that those who had been abused as children were more likely to also say they had experienced depression, anxiety, suicidal thoughts and to have engaged in self-harming behaviour than those who had not (Browne and Lim, 2008a).

As women are more likely to be survivors of sexual abuse, its impact may be greater on women in a relationship with a woman. Traumatic experiences of childhood sexual abuse are not unique to lesbian and bisexual women, yet few mental health professionals or social workers would assume that sexual abuse in childhood leads to heterosexuality. A survey participant in *Prescription for Change* provides a contrasting perspective:

> Mental health problems can be crippling, but when this involves being abused as a child it would be really nice if the first question you are asked is not: 'and do you think this is the reason why you prefer relationships with women?'. Sexuality is based on who you find attractive, not on what happened to you as a child. I find [questions of this kind to be] very negating of my identity. (Survey participant, unpublished data from Prescription for Change survey, 2008)

As a mental health social worker it is important to understand the meanings that service users attach to childhood sexual abuse and the impact they perceive it has in their life (if any), rather than assume that it has a causal role.

Exercise

The recovery star (see Figure 7.1) is a useful tool to help identify the mental health journey to recovery. Identify how Amiyah may be affected and how she might work towards better mental health in relation to each of the domains: trust and hope, managing mental health, self-care, living skills, social networks, work/education, relationships, addictive behaviour, responsibilities, and identity and self-esteem.

Figure 7.1: Recovery star

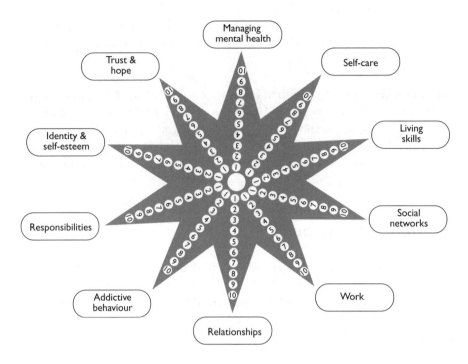

Source: DH (2009)

Introduction

Improving mental health and well-being has been identified as a priority for action in successive policy initiatives over the past two decades. A number of White Papers published by the Department of Health have recognised that mental health is as important as physical health and that as many as one in six people will have some sort of mental health problem in their life. These policy initiatives acknowledge that people with poor mental health are unable to fulfil their potential or play an active part in everyday life. Mental illness is not well understood; in the public mind, mental ill-health is equated with dangerousness and the stigma associated with mental health problems can be as debilitating as the illness itself. In efforts for tackling stigma and discrimination, the *National Service Framework 1999* explicitly set out to ensure that health and social services:

- Promote mental health for all, working with individuals and communities
- Combat discrimination against individuals and groups with mental health problems and promote social inclusion. (DH, 1999: 14)

Prior to these initiatives the then Labour government introduced its strategy for reform – *Modernising Mental Health Services* (DH, 1998) – which had three key aims of safe, sound and supportive services. Together, these reforms set out a comprehensive package of support to reduce mental health discrimination, combat social exclusion and provide accessible services to services users and their families and carers.

Historical background

Homosexuality was classified as a mental disorder in the Diagnostic and Statistical Manual (DSM II) until 1973 and in the World Health Organisation's International Classification of Diseases until it was removed in 1992. Lesbians, gay men and bisexual people were thought to be mentally ill by virtue of who they were and it was believed that same-sex attraction was a form of disease or psychopathology. In this view, homosexuality was not an identity but a developmental disorder. The belief that homosexuals were sick led to the search for a cure. Aversion therapy with electroconvulsive therapy (ECT) was the most common treatment used in NHS hospitals to convert LGBT people to heterosexuality (King et al, 2004). Although few mental health professionals would now consider being LGBT to be a mental illness, a number of LGBT people say that a professional made a causal link between their sexual orientation and their mental health problem (King et al, 2003).

Recent research has suggested that mental disorders are more common in LGBT people; they are more likely to experience psychological distress, to have thoughts of suicide and to self-harm (Warner et al, 2004). The legacy of pathology has meant that any discussion about mental health problems in LGBT communities is associated with the historic stigmatisation of LGBT identities. Some people argue that the suggestion of increased mental health problems among LGBT people fuels homophobia (Meyer, 2003). This argument confuses the classification of homosexuality as a mental disorder with concerns about the occurrence of mental health problems in LGBT communities. The first debate centres around questions about whether being LGBT is abnormal or a disease. The second discussion seeks to ascertain whether there are circumstances in LGBT people's everyday lives that may give rise to mental ill-health. In the past decade, there has been increasing research evidence to say that mental health problems may stem from experiences of discrimination and minority stress rather than as a result of being lesbian, gay or bisexual. The UK gay crime survey of 1,781 people found that twice as many people from black and minority ethnic (BME) backgrounds had experienced homophobic hate crime in the form of physical assault in comparison to all LGB people (8% versus 4%) (Dick, 2008). They were three and half times more likely to have experienced unwanted sexual contact.

For social workers and mental health professionals, it is important to understand the circumstances that may lead some LGBT people to have a higher risk of mental illness and to recognise the factors that contribute to mental well-being. With this knowledge, social workers can design effective interventions to promote recovery and improve mental health.

Underpinning knowledge

Experiences of discrimination

Experiences of prejudice and discrimination, such as racism, sexism or homophobia, may be associated with mental health problems. The increased likelihood of lifetime and day-to-day experiences of discrimination are more common among lesbians, gay men and bisexual people than their heterosexual counterparts (Mays and Cochran, 2001). Most of the research in suicide, however, has been conducted in the US among young people; less is known about suicide among adults. Experiences of homophobic bullying among young LGBT people have increasingly been documented (Hunt and Jensen, 2007). In one large-scale UK study, which compared the mental health of 1,093 heterosexuals with 1,284 lesbian, gay and bisexual people, almost a third of the LGBT people had attempted suicide (King et al, 2003). Two thirds of them said that experiences of discrimination, which included recent physical attack, verbal abuse and school bullying, were linked to their sexual orientation (Warner et al, 2004). These findings support those described in an earlier study conducted by the UK charity Childline, which revealed that in telephone calls from young LGBT people, some had thoughts of suicide because of their experiences of homophobic bullying (Childline, 2001).

Structural inequalities and social environments that devalue their lives, relationships and families are sources of stress, which may lead to psychological distress, deliberate self-harm (DSH) and thoughts of suicide (Warner et al, 2004). A recent survey of 2,199 heterosexual and 2,731 LGBT people undertaken by YouGov revealed that two thirds of LGBT people had experienced prejudice and discrimination related to their sexual orientation:

Around half of lesbians and gay men and a third of bisexual women and men reported that they had suffered stress. Around four in ten lesbians and gay men reported that they had been bullied, or felt frightened, and had suffered from low self-esteem. Around one in five gay men reported they had been physically assaulted and six per cent of lesbians that they had been sexually assaulted. Nine per cent of gay men and fourteen per cent of bisexual men reported a current mental health condition, as did 16 per cent of lesbians and over a quarter (26 per cent) of bisexual women. This contrasts sharply with just three per cent of heterosexual men and eight per cent of heterosexual women. (Ellison and Gunstone, 2009: 11)

Experiences of mental health services

Lesbian, gay and bisexual people are more likely to use mental health services and to have sought advice from their GP for emotional difficulties (King et al, 2003). Research suggests mixed experiences of mental health services ranging from excellent to extremely poor, including unhelpful reactions from mental health professionals (Glasgow Anti-Stigma Partnership, 2009). The anticipation of negative responses may lead to reluctance to access mental health services; in one study, this was the case for more than half of the LGBT participants (Stonewall Cymru, 2009). A Scottish study found poor experiences but these were attributed to a poor service generally rather than any specific link with sexual orientation (Glasgow Anti-Stigma Partnership, 2009).

Homophobia, such as physical attacks and abuse, has been recognised as a hate crime following the implementation of section 146 of the Crime and Disorder Act 2005. Since then, the Crown Prosecution Service (CPS) has collected annual data on the incidence of hate crime in England and Wales (CPS, 2009). The threat of violence extends beyond the immediate victims; many LGBT people are reluctant to show affection, such as holding hands, in public places for fear of eliciting unwanted attention. The fear of violence may impact on their quality of life and mental health.

Suicide among young people

Since the early 1990s, research has indicated a greater risk of suicidal behaviour among LGBT people than in the general population (Paul et al, 2002; King et al, 2007). Studies conducted in the US and the UK among young people have reported increased risk of suicide and suicidal ideation (Remafedi et al, 1998). Although it is not known whether there are more deaths from suicide, because sexual orientation is rarely included in post-mortem reports, those who attempt suicide on more than one occasion are more likely to 'succeed'. While social attitudes to sexual orientation in Western countries have changed dramatically since the decriminalisation of homosexuality in 1967, it was not until 2007 that discrimination on the grounds of sexual orientation was recognised in legislation. Suicide risk is a particular concern among young people who are coming to terms with their sexual orientation and forming a positive identity. A hostile social environment, violent assault in the home, degrading treatment by a family member or being forced to leave the family home are associated with high rates of suicide (Johnson et al, 2007). In the words of one young gay man, homophobic abuse at school led him to attempt suicide:

> Basically year 11 was the year when people started calling me gay a lot, queer boy, batty boy all these stupid names … every class I was going to it was happening and basically at this time, ah, we were having our mock exams and I just came out of an exam and went to the hall to find out when my next exam was going to be and ah, there was a group of people from my actual form who started with the name calling and that, and … some of them was slightly pushing and shoving, not great physical abuse or anything, mainly verbal abuse, but I was just trying to concentrate on my exams at the time and to have someone do that, it really got to me and … I felt, at the time, I felt I could stick up to them because so many of my friends said if someone does that to turn around and hit them and they'll go away and … I went to hit one of the lads but I just couldn't bring myself to do it and of course it just got even worse – they started more of the name calling, laughing at me and I kind of felt humiliated and ashamed … and I ended up running out of school and went home and I thought the only way of not having to go back was basically to kill myself and I basically took I think 56 tablets, mainly paracetamol but I was on anti-depressants at the time as well and I took of few of them and basically whatever tablets I could find in the house. (Johnson et al, 2007: 42)

The long-term impact on mental health

The experience of coming out in adolescence has a continuing long-term impact on mental health; those who had been subjected to homophobic bullying in school or were socially isolated were more likely to suffer poor mental health as adults (Rivers, 2004).

Self-harm

Suicide rates are lower among women than men in the general population; women are more likely to engage in practices of deliberate self-harm. In comparison to their heterosexual counterparts, lesbians are significantly more likely to have considered self-harm and bisexual women were the most likely to have done so (King et al, 2003). Lesbians and gay men were more likely than bisexual men and women to cite their sexual orientation as a reason for harming themselves; the researchers explain that self-harm has less to do with confusion about sexual orientation, but more with how to express themselves openly in society.

Psychological distress

Psychological distress, in particular, anxiety and depression, may be more common in lesbian, gay and bisexual people (King et al, 2007). Gay and bisexual men show higher rates of panic attacks and depression with symptoms occurring during early adolescence (Cochran and Mays, 2000). In comparison to heterosexual women, lesbian and bisexual women had higher rates of generalised anxiety disorder; those with depression were more likely to use prescription medication (Cochran et al, 2003).

Use of mental health services

'*Diagnosis Homophobic*' was the assessment given to mental health service provision in a study conducted by PACE, a mental health charity for LGBT people (MacFarlane, 1998). Users of mental health services reported that their identity was pathologised and they were fearful of heterosexism and homophobia from professionals and from other service users. They felt that not being out sometimes led to inappropriate care, and feelings of isolation sometimes contributed to internalised homophobia. A later study suggested that LGBT people may be more likely to use mental health services than their heterosexual counterparts (King et al, 2003). They indicated that problems in their encounters with mental health professionals ranged from instances of 'overt homophobia and discrimination, to a perceived lack of empathy' around sexual orientation (King et al, 2003: 5). Training is one of the report's key recommendations for social workers and mental health professionals to raise awareness of the relationship between sexual orientation and mental well-being and how to respond appropriately in a mental health setting. A service user who took part in the Prescription for Change survey said that staff are unwilling to tackle heterosexism and homophobia in mental health settings partly from a lack of confidence in talking about sexual orientation and partly because of a fear of association (ie by the very fact of raising issues to do with sexual orientation, people are often assumed to be lesbian, gay or bisexual). Another participant pointed to the exclusion of sexual orientation from diversity initiatives and that social policy might go some way towards making environments more inclusive:

> I run an independent mental health service user group and we are really aware that it doesn't feel possible to be out when using mental health services in particular. One of the biggest reasons for this continues to be staff discomfort with talking about sexuality. They continue to behave in heterosexist ways and do not challenge other people using services – or other staff – who make homophobic comments. Education and training – particularly run by people using services – and targets included in relevant Department of Health policies would help improve our experiences. (Survey participant, unpublished data, Prescription for Change survey, 2008)

What needs to improve?

In 2007. the National Institute for Mental Health England (NIMHE) said:

- ■ 'There is an urgent need for mental health services to develop LGBT sensitive services and an obvious initial step would be the incorporation of LGBT issues into diversity training for staff.'
- ■ 'An awareness of the mental health needs of LGBT people and their increased risk of mental disorders should become a standard part of training for health and social work professionals.'
- ■ 'Links with agencies and professionals who have particular expertise with gay and lesbian clients should be made and referrals to such agencies should be encouraged where appropriate' (King et al, 2007: 11).

Black and minority ethnic LGBT people and mental health

People tend to see BME communities as a homogeneous group with similar needs, attitudes and experiences. In the UK, BME communities include people who describe themselves as African-Caribbean, African, Middle Eastern, South Asian and South East Asian. There are many differences between ethnic minority groups because of different cultural and religious traditions, whether they are the first generation in their family living in the UK or long established, alongside differences in their experiences of racism and colonialism. There are also differences within communities – the place of religion in their lives, whether English is their first language and education.

BME LGBT people are disproportionately affected by homophobic violence, abuse and harassment (GALOP, 2001). In a study conducted in London, BME LGBT people were more likely to experience physical abuse, more likely to experience harassment from a stranger and equally likely to have experienced verbal abuse as their white LGBT counterparts.

There is little research about mental ill-health in BME LGBT communities in the UK and for this reason research undertaken in the US is considered here. One of the largest studies conducted among BME populations is the National Black Lesbian Needs Assessment, which was conducted in 2010 in the US with a sample of 1,596 women (Ramsey et al, 2010). It collected data on mental health, parenting, domestic violence and disclosure to health professionals. Experiences of homophobia, racism and social isolation have been linked to psychological distress: one study showed high levels of suicidal thoughts among Latino gay men (Diaz et al, 2001). Research conducted in Atlanta, Georgia, suggested that BME men may be disproportionately burdened by depressive distress and anxiety disorders in comparison to their white gay and BME heterosexual counterparts (Graham et al, 2009). Another study found that BME young gay and bisexual men reported higher levels of depression compared with their heterosexual counterparts; however, the group with the most compromised mental health were white young lesbian and bisexual women (Consalacion et al, 2004). The researchers concluded that it cannot be assumed that multiple minority identities are necessarily indicators for increased risk. A study by the leading UK mental health charity MIND, which included a subsample of BME participants, found that BME LGBT survey respondents were less likely than white respondents to have considered suicide (King and McKeown, 2003).

Comfort with sexual orientation/identity formation

Coming out, or the public acknowledgement of one's LGB identity, is said to indicate positive self-esteem and developmental maturity (Parks et al, 2004). Good mental health is associated with high levels of self-esteem, sustaining and enduring intimate relationships, and the ability to deal with adversity. Family plays a pivotal role in many BME communities, providing a resource to counter racism. In some communities, the needs of an individual are sometimes subsumed to the greater good of the whole family as a social and economic unit. This can mean that coming out is a complex process, sometimes to the whole family and sometimes to particular family members (siblings or mothers), while maintaining strong family ties. The barriers to coming out may be higher than for their white counterparts because the two aspects of their identity – BME and LGBT – are both disparaged in mainstream culture. Research in the US reports mixed findings about the strategies used by young black people. On the one hand, young BME lesbian, gay and bisexual people are less likely to be involved in LGBT social activities, they report less comfort with people knowing about their sexual orientation and they come out to fewer people than do white young people (Rosario et al, 2004a). Other findings suggest that BME LGBT people were younger when they began to question their sexual orientation, proceeded more slowly in making the decision and then disclosed their identity more quickly than their white counterparts (Parks et al, 2004).

Coming out and social networks

The expectation to publicly disclose one's sexual orientation presupposes favourable social conditions for coming out and finding similar others (Parks et al, 2004). Most LGBT people make decisions about coming out based on the degree of overlap or communication between audiences before coming out to any of them, and on whether their given audience (neighbourhoods, work colleagues, friends) is replaceable. BME social networks tend to be more extensive and seamless than white networks so that a degree of overlap between audiences is more likely. Given the smaller size of BME communities in the UK, black social networks may be less replaceable. The costs of coming out, then, may be greater for BME LGBT people than for their white counterparts (Parks et al, 2004).

There may also be differences within and between ethnic groups in patterns of disclosure and non-disclosure. In one study, a number of African-American gay men reported that while their families knew they were gay, many had never discussed it (Adams and Kimmel, 1997). Other study participants were more likely to have sexual contact only with other white men so that no one in their community would learn of their sexual orientation (Adams and Kimmel, 1997). In order to limit the number of people to whom they disclose, some black LGBs compartmentalise their identities.

Many BME LGBT people report experiences of racism in the LGBTcommunity; in one US study, 26% reported discomfort in spaces primarily attended by white people (Diaz et al, 2001). There have been recent reports of racial abuse in LGBT bars in the UK; Kam, a South Asian gay man, talked about the 'test kiss' requirement:

> Before we can go into a club bouncers ask us to kiss other men to prove we are really gay. White men are not asked to do this so I just don't bother going out anymore, it's not worth it. (Buttoo, 2010)

The experience of being rejected in public spaces was also revealed in a recent study which also found that BME men were objectified (McKeown et al, 2010). An Australian study found that South Asian gay men risked losing their connections with supportive BME networks if they were accepted in white LGBT spaces because of the processes of assimilation and the cultural distance they had to cover (Ridge et al, 1999; Mao et al, 2002).

The literature on LGBT identity development has almost universally proposed that psychological well-being is associated with the individual's self-perceptions as LGBT and the extent to which she or he has divulged their identity to others (Cass, 1979; Gerstel et al, 1989).

An extensive literature has developed to support people in becoming a 'healthy homosexual' and emphasis is placed on verbal disclosure, aptly illustrated in the title of one volume: *There Must Be 50 Ways to Tell Your Mother* (Sutcliffe, 1995). The corollary has been that people who are not out have been characterised as ashamed or guilty about their LGBT identity. Greene (2003) cautions against the tendency to presume that oppression is experienced in the same way for everyone who is LGBT or 'that it has the same meaning and consequences for them' (Greene, 2003: 358). Non-verbal disclosure may be more relevant in some BME communities, reflecting different understandings about identity. In some cultures, it is a process of becoming who they were meant to be (or already are); that is, a coming home or becoming rather than coming out (Walters and Person, 2008). An integrated model of identity development reflects some of the complexities of coming out as a BME LGBT person (Walters and Person, 2008).

In some cultures, there is little support for an individual public identity because the focus is upon the role one is expected to play in the family:

> A crucial distinction between traditional East Asian culture and Western culture is the concept of sexuality and sexual expression as a private matter. Any direct and open discussion of sexuality is unusual in East Asian cultures, as sexuality is considered to be a very sensitive subject. Even among one's closest friends, a discussion about sexuality is considered to be awkward and highly embarrassing at best, and at worst, is strictly taboo. (Chan, 1997: 244)

Coming out is a twofold process, which is seen to follow a prescribed pattern: coming out to others is the natural sequel to coming out to oneself. The assumption has often been that if someone is not able to publicly acknowledge their sexual orientation, then they have not accepted their LGBT identity. One study suggested that there were no significant differences in the sexual developmental milestones of sexual identity or sexual behaviour between BME and white young LGBT people (Rosario et al, 2004a). Of particular interest was the finding that

BME young people had greater increases in positive attitudes towards homosexuality and in certainty about their sexual identity over time than did white young people.

Coming out and the role of the family

In collectivist cultures, the family is an expression of social standing, in particular, its reputation and honour. Decisions about choosing a partner are not merely based upon meeting individual needs, but about a relationship that will bring benefit for both families (Greene, 1997). In some cultures, the family forms an economic unit that relies on traditional gender roles for the continuation of the family line. Family, then, plays an important role as a source of practical and emotional support and a bulwark against racism. Black lesbian and bisexual women may be more likely than white lesbian and bisexual women to maintain strong involvements with their families, to have children, to have continued contact with men and their heterosexual peers, and to depend on family members for support (Greene, 1997).

Although there are restrictions on the disclosure of sexual orientation, in some cultures, there is more fluidity in the ways in which sexuality can be expressed; for example, there may be a greater acceptance of two men holding hands or public displays of affection between men than might be tolerated in many white communities.

For some BME LGBT people, there is a degree of dissonance between their racial and sexual identity (Bhugra, 1997). In one of the earliest UK studies, South Asian gay men made concerted attempts at concealment and were likely to hide their sexual identity from work colleagues by acting straight, talking about girls, asking female friends to ring them at work and using other smokescreens (Bhugra, 1997). These issues are a continuing concern for South Asian LGBT people; recent media attention has highlighted the practice of entering a marriage of convenience to avoid being disowned or to circumvent family pressure for a heterosexual marriage (Puri, 2008). But there is also regret among South Asian gay men at being unable to fulfil family expectations for marriage and children:

> All my family are aware [that I am gay], but my parents, or more so my mum, denies it to herself regularly. I'm the only boy in the family, so my 'Asian' duty is to continue the family lineage ... I do feel like there is no space in a culture that is so 'marriage and children' focused. (McKeown et al, 2010: 847)

A London study found that South Asian people were far less likely than those from other ethnic groups to be open about their sexual identity to anyone but their close friends. For instance, only 27% of Asian respondents were open to their mothers about their sexual identity compared to 61% of African-Caribbean respondents (Galop, 2001).

A recent study of BME gay and bisexual men revealed that some had come out to their families and, instead of support and protection, they felt betrayed: 'So at every family event or any function you are the person they all look at, like that is the gay boy, and you just have to deal with it' (Daniel, in Graham et al, 2009: 277). Other participants felt abandoned by their families because they did not conform to cultural notions about black masculinity.

Minority stress

The concept of minority stress has been used to explain the increased likelihood of mental health problems among LGBT people. Minority stress is precipitated by conditions in the social environment that lead to dislocation from social structures, norms and institutions. It includes the 'experience of prejudice events, expectations of rejection, hiding and concealing, internalized homophobia and ameliorative coping strategies' (Meyer, 2003: 674). Meyer (2003) argues that minority stress does not lead to increased mental health problems in BME people due to growing up in a self-enhancing social environment where strategies to deal with racism may be learned and where BME people develop a positive self-identity in a supportive family environment (Meyer, 2003). Rates of suicide among BME men in London have been found to be lower than their white counterparts if they lived in relatively high-density ethnic communities; the opposite was the case if they did not (Pritchard, 2006). This finding appears to suggest that it may be communities as much as families that provide the necessary social environment to deal with prejudice and discrimination.

Survival and resilience

Despite findings which suggest that suicidal behaviour is higher among LGBT people, it is not sexual orientation per se that increases the risk of suicide, but rather the extent to which the young person is socially and emotionally supported (Rutter and Soucar, 2002). The experience of coming out in a supportive environment of family and friends is vital to achieving a positive identity as an LGBT young person and self-acceptance (see Chapter 4 on young people). Poor mental health among LGBT people is linked with feelings of being different and not conforming to stereotypical notions of masculinity and femininity, homophobic bullying at school, high levels of stress, lifetime abuse, physical or verbal attack, and substance abuse (Rivers, 2004).

Building social capital and connectedness is important in preventing mental health problems among LGBT people. Community-based facilities offer a means of developing a sense of belonging and the opportunity to establish relationships with peers not only in adolescence, but throughout the lifetime.

Policy context

The National Suicide Prevention Strategy for England 2002 aimed to reduce suicide in groups who are at high risk of taking their own life. Four inclusion criteria were applied:

- a known statistical risk of suicide;
- actual numbers of suicides in the group were known;
- evidence exists on which to base preventative measures;
- effective monitoring of preventive measures exist. (King et al, 2007: 3)

LGBT people were not included in Goal 1 of the strategy as a high-risk group (which means that interventions would be targeted specifically to them) because they did not meet these criteria. Routine data collection and monitoring of the number of suicides among LGBT people is not possible because sexual orientation is not recorded when the death is registered. Moreover, Coroners' Courts are more likely to pass an open verdict on cause of death. A systematic review of the worldwide literature was commissioned by the National Institute of Mental Health England, which showed that LGBT people are at significantly higher risk of mental disorder, thoughts of suicide, substance misuse and deliberate self-harm than heterosexual people (King et al, 2007). Following publication of the review, LGBT people were included under Goal 2.8 in the National Suicide Prevention Strategy as a group with specific needs (NMHDU, 2008).

The equivalent policy document in Scotland – 'Choose life: a national strategy and action plan to prevent suicide' – does include sexual orientation as a risk for individuals and recognises that the quality of response from services and actions to prevent suicide should be sensitive to the needs of LGBT people (Scottish Government, 2002: 47). The Welsh Assembly document 'Talk to me: a national plan to reduce suicide and self harm in Wales 2008–2013' (Welsh Assembly, 2009) does not include sexual orientation.

The Code of Practice for the Mental Health Act 1983 (2008) identified five guiding principles that should be taken into account when making decisions about a course of action. The respect principle emphasises that practitioners must:

> recognise and respect the diverse needs, values and circumstances of each patient, including their race, religion, culture, gender, age, sexual orientation and any disability. They must consider the patient's views, wishes and feelings (whether expressed at the time or in advance), so far as they are reasonably ascertainable, and follow those wishes wherever practicable and consistent with the purpose of the decision. There must be no unlawful discrimination. (DH, 2008: p 5, section 1.4)

Recent research suggests that psychological distress, self-harm and suicide attempts may be linked to experiences of discrimination (Mays and Cochran, 2001; King et al, 2003); this contrasts with earlier studies that attributed mental ill-health to sexual orientation. It is important to note that the majority of LGBT people do not experience mental health problems. Factors such as positive experiences of coming out, family support, social connectedness and the existence of role models contribute to emotional and psychological resilience.

Conclusion

This chapter has discussed some of the key issues in social work practice and mental health with lesbian, gay and bisexual people. Research suggests that, in comparison to their heterosexual counterparts, LGBT people may be more at risk of mental health problems and thoughts of suicide (King et al, 2007). This increased risk has been historically attributed to unhappiness about having a stigmatised identity: that is, being LGBT causes mental health problems. Current research challenges these myths and stereotypes: experiences of homophobic bullying in adolescence, discrimination in adulthood and concerns about disclosure may lead to increased vulnerability for poor mental health (Mays and Cochran, 2001). Understanding mental health concerns can inform person-centred planning and the Care Programme Approach in social work practice with LGBT people.

Further reading

Glasgow Anti-Stigma Partnership (2009) '*There's More to Me': A Report on Lesbian, Gay and Bisexual People's Beliefs, Attitudes and Experiences in Mental Health,* Glasgow: Scottish Association for Mental Health.

King, M., Smith, G. and Bartlett, A. (2004) 'Treatments of homosexuality in Britain since the 1950s – An oral history: the experience of professionals', *British Medical Journal,* 328(7437), 420–9.

Laird, N. (2004) *Community Engagement with LGBT Mental Health Service Users in the South Side of Glasgow. Glasgow: Inclusion* – Glasgow demonstration project.

McNamee, H. (2006) *Out On Your Own: An Examination of the Mental Health of Young Same-sex Attracted Men,* Belfast: The Rainbow Project. Available at: www.rainbow-project.org

Morrison, C. and Mackay, A. (2000) *The Experience of Violence and Harassment of Gay Men in the City of Edinburgh,* Edinburgh: Scottish Executive Social Research.

NMHDU (National Mental Health Development Unit) (2008) *National Suicide Prevention Strategy: Annual progress 2008.* Available at: http://www.nmhdu.org.uk/silo/files/national-suicide-prevention-strategy-for-england--annual-report-on-progress-2008.pdf (accessed 24 November 2009).

Robinson, A. and Williams, M. (2003) *Counted Out: The Findings from the 2002–2003 Survey Stonewall Cymru of Lesbian, Gay and Bisexual People in Wales.*, Cardiff: Stonewall Cymru.

Scottish Government (2002) *Choose Life: A National Strategy and Action Plan to Prevent Suicide.* Available at: http://www.scotland.gov.uk/Resource/Doc/46932/0013932.pdf (accessed 13 July 2010).

Welsh Assembly (2009) *Talk to Me: A National Plan to Reduce Suicide and Self harm in Wales (2008–2013).* Available at: http://wales.gov.uk/consultations/healthsocialcare/talktome/?lang=en (accessed 13 July 2010).

Disability

Practice scenario

Kate is a 31-year-old woman with a degenerative condition that necessitates using a wheelchair. She lives in the family home with her mother and brother in a rural area. Her mother works part-time as a cleaner and her brother stacks shelves in the nearby supermarket. Her benefits bring her a greater income than either her mother or brother earn and she feels guilty about this. The family have no transport. She has recently come out to her social worker as lesbian but she does not want her family to know. Her condition means that it is likely she will live only another five years and she would like to meet other women.

Questions

This chapter discusses some of the issues experienced by people with physical and learning disabilities who are lesbian, gay, bisexual or trans. Consider the following questions as you read the chapter to inform the knowledge, skills and values that underpin your social work practice with Kate:

- ➲ What is your understanding about the issues facing Kate?
- ➲ What are the potential resources available to support her?
- ➲ How would you use social work theories to explore what she wants in the last years of her life?
- ➲ How would you work with her to take account of social work values and codes of practice?
- ➲ How can you support her to live a life in a way that sustains her?

Introduction

The medical model has formed the traditional approach to disability (Brothers, 2003). The approach defines disabled people by their health condition – by what they are not able to do – rather than their abilities.

It is sometimes known as the individual model because it promotes the view that the disability is the responsibility of the individual and that an individual disabled person should fit in to the way that society is organised; the problem is with the individual disabled person not with society. It assumes that a disabled person is dependent and needs to be cured or cared for. Consequently, disabled people's lives have often been regulated by health and social care professionals who make decisions about disabled people's lives without fully consulting with them or offer limited choices. Medical diagnoses are used to determine access to welfare, housing, education, leisure and employment.

By contrast, the social model of disability, which was developed through the Disabled People's Movement, offers a politicised approach to understanding disability (Gillespie-Sells et al, 1998). It considers that discrimination and prejudice in society limit the life chances of disabled people. Disability is the disadvantage a person experiences that results from the barriers they encounter in their everyday lives, including the attitudes of professionals and the general public, inaccessible environments, and organisational barriers. It is the removal of these barriers that is necessary to ensure that disabled people are able to take an active role in society. In the words of one social worker, the social model:

> is very much around being about people not patients; it's being about practice that is built around the person; it's about an holistic approach to meeting that person's needs; it's hopefully about the individual themselves needing … a kind of definition of the outcomes that they're looking for; the support that they need to help them to achieve that. (Rainbow Ripples, 2006: 73)

For people with learning disabilities, the medical model meant that many people lived in seclusion in long-stay hospitals, which were closed in the decade up to the early 1990s (Shakespeare et al, 1996). The social model led to living arrangements based on integration and inclusion in the community. Tom Shakespeare (2002) offers a critique of the dichotomised understanding of the medical and social approaches to disability.

Policy and legislation

Over the past two decades, a number of legislative changes have sought to begin to address the discrimination experienced by disabled people in their everyday lives. The Disability Discrimination Act 1995 made it unlawful to discriminate against disabled people in employment and in the provision of goods, services and facilities. The legislation defines disability and a disabled person as someone who 'has a physical or mental impairment which has a substantial and long-term adverse effect on his [sic] ability to carry out normal day-to-day activities' (DDA 1995, section 1.1). This definition is reiterated in the Equality Act 2010 (for further discussion, see Chapter 2).

The UN Convention on the Rights of Persons with Disabilities (UNCRPD) marked a paradigm shift in attitudes and approaches to disability when it was adopted in 2006. The convention, which was ratified by the UK government in 2009, became the first human rights treaty of the 21st century and promotes a view of disabled people as subjects who are entitled to enjoy human rights and fundamental freedoms.

Introduced in 2001, *Valuing People* (DH, 2001b) was the first policy initiative for 30 years for people with learning disabilities in England and Wales (a similar initiative was introduced in Scotland with the aim of promoting social inclusion). Valuing People aimed to support people to live full lives and play an active role in society and ensure that the things that non-learning disabled people take for granted, including a home, access to transport, the ability to take part in leisure activities, employment and developing intimate and personal relationships, are within the reach of people with learning disabilities. Valuing People was significant because it outlined a new approach to providing services with and for people with learning disabilities based on four key principles:

Rights
- People with learning disabilities have the right to a decent education, to vote, to marry and have a family, and to express their opinions, with help and support to do so where necessary.
- All public services will treat people with learning disabilities as individuals with respect for their dignity, and challenge discrimination on all grounds including disability.

Independence
- Promoting independence is a key aim for the Government's modernisation agenda.
- People's individual needs will differ, the starting presumption should be one of independence, rather than dependence, with public services providing the support needed to maximise this.
- Independence in this context does not mean doing everything unaided.

Choice
- People with learning disabilities want a real say in where they live, what work they should do and who looks after them.

- For too many people with learning disabilities, these are currently unattainable goals.
- Everyone should be able to make choices. This includes people with severe and profound disabilities who, with the right help and support, can make important choices and express preferences about their day-to-day lives.

Inclusion
- Being part of the mainstream is something most of us take for granted. We go to work, look after our families, visit our GP, use transport, go to the swimming pool or cinema. Inclusion means enabling people with learning disabilities to do those ordinary things, make use of mainstream services and be fully included in the local community. (DH, 2001b: 23–4)

The policy sought to enable people and their families to have a greater say in what services would be delivered and more choice and control through direct payments in how care would be organised. *Putting People First* (DH, 2007) took this agenda forward and confirmed the shift to increasing personalisation of services, including person-centred approaches and individual budgets.

In 2009, *Valuing People Now* (HMG, 2009) was introduced in recognition that much work remained to be done: people with learning disabilities are among those groups who are most socially excluded in society, few have employment or a home of their own, they are often the target of hate crime and they experience inequalities in access to healthcare. *Valuing People Now* acknowledged the importance of relationships in people's lives, including the right to have a civil partnership.

The following legislation and guidance are also relevant in the context of disabled people's care:

- NHS and Community Care Act 1990
  - Section 3: provision of community care services.
  - Section 47: requires the local authority to provide an assessment.
- Community Care (Direct Payments) Act 1996
- Mental Capacity Act 2005
- Safeguarding Adults 2005 – This practice guidance sets out the framework for the protection of adults (including older people, those with mental illness, physical or learning disability) from harm; financial, sexual or emotional abuse; or neglect.
- 2010 White Paper: *A Vision for Adult Social Care: Capable Communities and Active Citizens* (DH, 2010c) – Individuals not institutions take control of their care. Personal budgets, preferably as direct payments, are provided

to all eligible people. Information about care and support is available for all local people, regardless of whether or not they fund their own care.

Person-centred planning

Person-centred planning (PCP) replaces previous models of care planning where decisions were made about people's lives without their involvement. PCP is an approach derived from the shared values of *Valuing People* and the social model of disability and helps to identify a person's needs, wants, hopes and dreams and seeks to find ways of achieving them by placing the person, and their circle of support, at the centre of decisions about life planning. It uses visual methods, such as maps and paths, to illustrate the person's goals and identifies clear ways of achieving them.

Underpinning knowledge

Identity development and coming out

Practice in social care with people with learning disabilities has tended to restrict opportunities for sexual relationships and this has been even more the case for same-sex relationships. Many people with learning disabilities see their sexual orientation as an important part of their identity, but the attitudes of the people they live with can present a barrier to its expression or fulfilment (Abbott and Howarth, 2005). One man reported that it was not until his parents died when he was in his fifties that he was able to acknowledge to himself that he was gay (Beyond Barriers, 2002). People may be reluctant to come out to their family for fear of being rejected or facing family disapproval; this may be especially the case when they rely on carers for practical support and the loss of the relationship would be significant. In a groundbreaking study, *Secret Loves, Hidden Lives,* which asked people with learning disabilities about their first feelings and coming out, many said that they knew they were LGBT from an early age and tried to suppress their feelings or 'blank [them] out'; as children and young people, few knew the words to describe their feelings (Abbott and Haworth, 2005: 8). A number had waited for some time before telling anyone about their sexual orientation and were anxious about being rejected.

In the Rainbow Ripples study, members of staff appeared to be more concerned about how other residents would react to knowing that someone was LGBT rather than supporting them to come out. When asked whether he had come out to other residents, one person was explicitly told that he should not do so:

> Errm, no definitely not. I was told to shut up about the whole issue [their sexual orientation] a couple of years ago … I was told that … the other residents … *(laughs)*, might not know how to cope with somebody who was actually in a gay sexual relationship. (Rainbow Ripples, 2006: 114)

There are also perceptions that LGBT people do not use social care services or that they must conform to a particular stereotype of what an LGBT person should look like. Because LGBT communities are often dispersed rather than located in a geographic community, a service user who is LGBT may be the only LGBT person to use the service. This may be an additional barrier to coming out for BME LGBT people who are often presumed to be heterosexual:

> It is unthinkable of telling a member of staff that you are LGBT. Especially where you seem to be the only LGBT using the service. I suspect even staff are afraid. Especially in the Asian community. (Asian gay man, a family carer for a learning disabled relative, in CSCI, 2008: 9)

People were more likely to have experienced negative rather than positive responses from staff and services. One man was asked to leave his group home when they found out he was gay and two lesbians with learning disabilities said they were repeatedly rebuked if they showed any physical affection towards each other (Abbott and Howarth, 2005). Yet, despite these reactions, people in the *Secret Loves, Hidden Lives* study were more likely to be out to social care workers or other professionals than to family or friends. However, most were out to only a small number of staff that they trusted and who they believed would be accepting of them. Perhaps because of the potential key role that social care workers can play in people's lives, there was as much emotion involved in coming out to staff as there was to family. Having a positive reaction brought a sense of relief and feelings of being less alone.

Disabled people are more likely to be socially isolated and less likely to have close friends than their non-disabled peers. Establishing a friendship network is an important part of developing and expressing one's sexual orientation, but there are a number of barriers to meeting other LGBT people. Non-disabled people have a wider choice of places to meet others through educational settings, work and leisure activities. Knowing where to meet other LGBT people was often the first difficulty; personal assistants, support workers and social workers were often not familiar with LGBT venues or comfortable in attending them. For one participant in the Rainbow Ripples study, the internet, which they used in their bedroom, was virtually the only access they had to the LGBT community because their carers were 'unwilling to acknowledge their sexual orientation' or assist them in their desire to meet and talk to other LGBT people (Rainbow Ripples, 2006: 128). Another participant explained that some professionals did not understand that socialising with other LGBT people, attending events like Pride, going to the theatre or films, or accessing LGBT literature form an important part of LGBT culture:

> And they [social workers and carers] don't take into account that we are a community, that disabled lesbians and gay men are a community. That we have a culture of our own. That they need to recognise that culture in the same way that they recognise the BME community and their culture. (Rainbow Ripples, 2006: 148)

By contrast, a social care worker who took part in the *Secret Loves, Hidden Lives* study talked about the key role staff can play in offering support and in recognising that culture is also a collection of social mores, values and behaviours:

> There is so much more to his perception of being gay … he wants recognition that this is part of him. This is a part of a cultural identity he wants to explore. To be part of a culture you have to be supported in it and you have to learn the codes and behaviours. You are not going to be able to enter that unless you have support. (Abbot and Howarth, 2005: 44)

Getting to venues can pose problems as many people do not have their own vehicle; many people may worry about possible abuse and discrimination when using public transport. Paying for transport was another barrier. Non-disabled LGBT people often ask taxis to drop them off a few streets away from a gay venue to keep their identity hidden from taxi-drivers, but this may not be a solution for everyone (Rainbow Ripples, 2006). Many people needed to travel some distance into a city and had to return home early while the bars were still quiet and this also restricted their opportunities for social interaction (Abbott and Howarth, 2005). Good practice in this area would be to take account of the specific need to travel distances to meet up with friends. This was the situation for one disabled lesbian:

> The Independent Living Fund did consider my needs for social interaction within the lesbian community, and with my wider 'lesbian family', and gave me extra hours to be able to go and see friends who live on the other side of London. I think this is because they understand independent living in its real sense. (CSCI, 2008: 9)

There can be challenges in accessing social spaces, but there are also attitudinal barriers. The youth-oriented culture, narrowly defined conceptions of body image, a busy, noisy environment, and the use of recreational drugs serve to alienate disabled LGBT people and prevent them from meeting others (Ellis, 1995). For one gay man, the emphasis on physical appearance made him feel awkward and conspicuous:

> I think in the scene [a term used to refer collectively to spaces where LGBT people socialise] people tend to look at appearance first, and if they see someone attractive then they'll sort of go from there. When I'm on the scene people tend to look at the wheelchair and not the person sat in it. Which is frustrating. I've never picked anyone up on the scene since I've been in a wheelchair, and I've put that down to the fact that I'm in a wheelchair. It's a purely physical thing. (Molloy et al, 2003: 68)

Personal and sexual relationships

The intersection of disability and sexual orientation presents a double-bind: homosexuality is considered to be a sexualised identity and one that is inherently dangerous while people with disabilities are widely believed to be asexual. Despite recognition of the importance of sex for self-esteem and a self-determined life, disabled people are not only perceived to be asexual, but also frequently compelled to be so. There are a number of preconceptions about disabled people's sexuality: all sex is heterosexual; only independently functioning disabled people can handle sexual relations; and beliefs whereby disabled people are suspended in childhood (Brothers, 2003). Society also enforces compulsory celibacy by denying disabled people access to relevant and appropriate sex education. In one study, only 28% of disabled women who had attended special schools had received sex education and those who were born disabled were much less likely to receive sex education than those who became disabled (Gillespie-Sells et al, 1998). Many disabled people internalise these assumptions, believing that sex is 'naughty' and not for them (Brothers, 2003: 52). The consequences of ignoring the possibilities of a same-sex sexual relationship may mean that people are more susceptible to abuse.

It is often assumed that the act of coming out is a sexual declaration and concerns about vulnerability have been uppermost in the minds of carers rather than pleasure and fulfilment. As with heterosexual relationships for people with learning disabilities, there are issues about consent, mental capacity and risk. But while parents, carers and professionals are concerned to protect learning disabled people from exploitation, this concern often means that people are not empowered to lead the lives they would choose. Previous research has found that for people with learning disabilities, love was a major topic of conversation in research interviews; moreover, relationships featured strongly in people's hopes and dreams for the future (Abbott and Howarth, 2005). The possibility for a satisfying sexual relationship is something that most people take for granted; but for disabled LGBT people, there is an expectation of compulsory celibacy. Sex and intimacy are not seen as basic needs for a disabled person, but as luxury desires (Valios, 2001). People with physical disabilities felt that their sexuality was viewed as 'repulsive' by others:

> I feel society does not look at disabled people as sexual beings ... if you're disabled they don't expect you to have sexuality or want a physical relationship, which is quite hard.... They don't think you're capable, they sometimes don't feel you have emotions and feelings like everyone else, for a disabled person to be sexual and a lesbian, then God, that is outrageous! (Molloy et al, 2003: 55)

The perception that disabled LGBT people neither want nor need intimate relationships forms a powerful backdrop that they must negotiate when they seek to form a partnership.

Deaf LGBT people

Being deaf is often assumed to simply mean to be without hearing, but the use of the capitalised term Deaf refers to people who identify themselves as members of a linguistic minority who use British Sign Language (BSL) and who positively identify themselves as belonging to a discrete cultural group – the Deaf community (Taylor and Bishop, 2000). Despite this politicised identity, there has been very little research into their health and social care needs. The *Count Me In* study, which was conducted in Brighton and Hove, revealed experiences of bullying, abuse and exclusion from services. The 28 Deaf participants were much less likely than others in the study to say that they found it easy to be an LGBT person:

> There's the [local] Deaf Association ... but I wouldn't go there because it's a very church-led organisation ... and has a real sort of history of being quite discriminatory against LGBT people ... they're the service, the provider that the council would first look to if they wanted to access the deaf community for [OurCity], and yet they're not welcoming for LGBT people. (Browne, 2009: 2)

Sinecka (2008) provides an account of a young Deaf gay man who developed pride in his Deaf community, but struggled to identify as a gay man because of the lack of family support and the size of his local community. David Nyman (2000) estimates that there are approximately 500 Deaf LGBT people with specific groups offering advice and support in cities throughout the UK including Brighton, Newcastle, Leicester, Nottingham, London, Derby, Glasgow and Wales. Deaf LGBT people have lobbied the national organisation, the British Deaf Association, to include LGBT people in their equal opportunities policy. Deaf LGBT people have organised workshops on HIV and sexual health, counselling and befriending, where deaf LGBT people themselves have acted as trainers (Nyman, 2000).

Disability hate crime and discrimination

Disability hate crime was legally recognised as a crime of a serious nature by section 146 of the Criminal Justice Act 2003. Unlike crimes motivated by race or religious hatred, the Act did not create a new offence, but imposed a duty on courts to increase the sentence where it could be shown that the crime was motivated by hostility towards someone with a disability. The legislation does not apply to crimes committed because of the perceived vulnerability of the victim, for example, the theft of a wallet from a blind person. Statistics for disability hate crime have only been collected by the Crown Prosecution Service (CPS) since 2007. A report produced by the Organization for Security and Co-operation in Europe (OSCE) found that '1,476 crimes motivated by bias' against people with disabilities were recorded by the CPS in England and Wales in 2008/09 (OSCE, 2009: 82). Of these, only 393 people were prosecuted under the disability hate crime legislation, which amounts to 3% of the total number of all hate crime prosecutions. There is evidence to suggest that a disproportionate number of disabled people are repeat victims of anti-social behaviour. Official figures, then, do not indicate that disabled people are at risk; instead, evidence about the prevalence of hate crime has been documented by disability rights groups.

A recent report, *Getting Away with Murder* (Quarmby, 2008), provides evidence that disabled people are harassed and verbally abused and that some have even been subject to torture or murdered. The report presents details of the deaths of 18 people that are attributable to hate crime. Previous research suggests that hate crimes often take place in public spaces, which may be isolated such as in the street or in a park, but also in places where it would be expected that the presence of others would deter abuse or violence such as in sports centres, cafes or shops (National Disability Authority, 2005). The study also found that 20% of people had been attacked on public transport. Supporting evidence was produced by *Disability Now* magazine in its hate crime dossier, which considered 51 crimes committed against disabled people where only one was investigated as a disability hate crime. Abbott and Howarth (2005) found that half of the learning disabled LGBT people who took part in their study had been physically or verbally abused by strangers. Hate crime has a negative impact on people's sense of security and well-being; they feel that they are not able to participate in society as equal citizens. Disabled people may be less likely to report crime because of a lack of confidence in the criminal justice system. When asked whether they believed that offenders would be brought to justice, only 35% agreed in comparison to 41% of the general population (Quarmby, 2008).

Personal narrative

Shirley Leggott, a 37-year-old woman with a learning disability, wrote about her experiences of coming out as a lesbian in *The Guardian* and the support she received from the staff where she lived in Mencap-supported accommodation. Her account highlights many of the issues considered in this chapter and underlines the reasons that the support she received was so crucial in the development of her identity:

> Soon after moving here I made the decision to 'come out'. I'd known I was gay for quite some time but did not have the courage to tell anyone. Most people seemed to be only interested in my disability.

> Mencap staff were great. They assured me that I was perfectly normal and promised to support me in any way they could. That was a weight off my mind.

> I then decided to come out to everyone else, including my family, which wasn't very easy for me. But the staff were behind me all the way to support me through my 'ordeal', which is what it felt like.

> That was just the start of my journey. I then wanted to get to know other gay people. Staff helped me to access a support group for gay women, support groups for gay disabled women, and any other connections they could think of.

> They travelled with me to various venues until I had the confidence to go alone. In fact they must have been sick of me. My need to meet people, or that 'special person', was my big desire. It was also very hard to achieve.

Since coming out, I have gone through some very difficult times emotionally, and I have made a lot of mistakes and taken a few risks along the way. But at least I have had the opportunity to make my mistakes and take those risks without being made to feel childish or silly. Staff have supported me through my mistakes as well as my achievements. (Leggott, 2005: 13)

Developing good practice in assessments and person-centred planning

The personalisation agenda in adult social care will ensure that services are relevant for many users, including LGBT people. Good practice will draw on principles of person-centred planning and self-directed services:

■ Make sure that the introductory information, such as the organisation's statement of purpose and service user guide, is positive around issues of sexual orientation and gender identity. This means that LGBT people will be more confident in coming out at assessment.

■ Be clear about the confidentiality of the assessment at the start. Who else will see the assessment? This helps LGBT people decide whether they want to come out or not.

■ Introduce an element of self-assessment that includes open questions. This enables LGBT people to decide whether to come out themselves, rather than waiting for an appropriate time to raise the issue in a verbal assessment.

■ Ensure questions do not assume that people are heterosexual, for example, replace questions about 'husband or wife' with 'partner' and avoid the phrase 'marital status'.

■ Use open questions that enable people to describe who is important to them and their lifestyle, without pressuring people into giving answers, for example, 'Would you like to tell us who are the important people in your life?'.

Potential questions for self-assessment

■ Do you need support to keep up contact with anyone in particular?
■ How do you like to spend your leisure time?
■ Do you need support to be involved with any groups or activities?
■ Is there anything you would like to tell us about what is important to you in your life? (CSCI, 2008: 15)

Personal support plan

Using the hopes and dreams table (see Table 8.1 in the exercise below):

- How can you best elicit the hopes and dreams of a service user with learning disabilities?
- Think about who is in their 'circle of support'.
- What is important to them?

Exercise: personal support plans

Use the Table 8.1 to identify your own hopes and dreams. In each of the four boxes of the table, produce a picture of what each of these might be.

Table 8.1: Identifying hopes and dreams with people with learning disabilities

Hopes and dreams	Things I like about me
Things that are important to me	Things I'm good at

Conclusion

In the *Secret Loves, Hidden Lives* research, people felt that the emotional and practical support needed to develop a same-sex relationship should be considered to be part of a social worker's role (Abbott and Howarth, 2005). People valued staff who were open, non-judgemental and who made time to talk about issues of concern to them. Some service providers had taken a proactive role and had displayed pictures showing same-sex couples. One man was helped by staff in his home to fill in order forms for gay DVDs; another was put in touch with a support group for LGBT people with learning disabilities.

Resources

The following resources were developed from the *Secret Loves, Hidden Lives* research project for people with learning disabilities. They are available at: http://www.bristol.ac.uk/norahfry/resources/online/

- Phil's story': a photo-story about a gay man with learning difficulties.
- 'Jan's story': a photo-story about a lesbian with learning difficulties.
- 'Challenging homophobia and heterosexism' – a booklet for people with learning difficulties and the staff that support them.
- A resource pack containing information, ideas and training suggestions about sexuality designed to be used by staff working with people with learning difficulties.

Further reading

Avante Consulting (2006) *On Safe Ground: LGBT Disabled People and Community Groups*, Edinburgh: The Equality Network.

Browne, K. (2009) *Count Me In: Deaf LGBT Lives*, Brighton: University of Brighton and Spectrum.

Brothers, M. (2003) 'Not just ramps and Braille: disability and sexual orientation', in K.E. Zappone (ed) *Re-thinking Identity: The Challenge of Diversity*, Dublin: Joint Equality and Human Rights Forum, pp 49–64. Available at: http://www.ihrc.ie (accessed 26 February 2007).

CPS (Crown Prosecution Service) (2007) *Disability Hate Crime: Policy for Prosecuting Cases*, London: CPS.

Droy, R. (2010) *Diversity Toolkit Focussed on LGBT People*, Southampton: Centre for Independent Living.

Gillespie-Sells, K., Hill, M. and Robbins, B. (eds) (1998) *She Dances to Different Drums: Research into Disabled Women's Sexuality*, London: King's Fund.

Leggott, S. (2005) '"Out" and about', *The Guardian*, 22 June, p 13.

Molloy, D., Knight, T. and Woodfield, K. (2003) *Diversity in Disability: Exploring the Interactions between Disability, Ethnicity, Age, Gender and Sexuality, Research Report 188*, London: Department for Work and Pensions.

OSCE (Organization for Security and Co-operation in Europe) (2009) 'Hate crimes in the OSCE region'. Available at: osce.org (accessed 22 December 2009).

Quarmby, K. (2008) *Getting Away with Murder: Disabled People's Experiences of Hate Crime*, London: Scope.

Substance misuse

Practice scenario

I started taking a lot of drugs on a regular basis, from about the age of seventeen onwards. I was becoming more and more mentally unbalanced. Because I hadn't come out to anybody. And I was extremely confused about what I was supposed to do about my sexuality. I suppose that's another reason why I was taking a lot of drugs. I was trying to escape from that in some way. Not that drugs are a direct escape from coming to terms with your sexuality. But it does maybe help unblock your sexual drive. Especially if it's ... if you ... if there is nowhere to put it to use. I think what I was confused about really was that, it wasn't whether or not I was gay. (Ahmed, young gay man, in Keogh et al, 2009: 17)

Questions
- What are your learning objectives as a social worker in your work with Ahmed?
- Identify the focus of your enquiry.
- What resources and people can support your work with him?
- What are the potential alternative courses of action?

Introduction

Substance misuse became a key area for social policy in the early 21st century where it was linked to a number of social problems including criminal activity, unemployment and anti-social behaviours. Misusing drugs applies to legal substances, such as alcohol, or illegal substances, like cannabis or cocaine. In the popular imagination, people who misuse substances are often seen to be the agents of their own problems and are believed to be ambivalent about changing their behaviour. For many people who are dependent on substances, the greatest harm is not to others, but to themselves. The impact on the body of excessive alcohol includes cirrhosis of the liver, cardiovascular problems, the destruction of brain cells, increased risk of cancer and diabetes, malnutrition, and sexual problems. Many people use substances to enhance pleasurable experiences; others come to rely on them as a mechanism for coping with life's challenges, often from a young age, and substance use can lend a temporary boost in self-esteem or social confidence. Drug use becomes misuse when someone becomes dependent or the use becomes problematic or harmful to themselves or others. Many people use drugs on a regular basis while maintaining their employment and continuing to effectively parent their children.

Policy and legislation

Drugs have formed a key focus for government intervention with four policy initiatives since the mid-1990s. Central to the policy objectives of *Drugs: Protecting Families and Communities 2008–2011* (Home Office, 2008) was the recognition that best outcomes could only be achieved if the needs of members of all communities were taken into account. It noted that some groups were under-represented in treatment or access to other services and providers should understand the nature and level of need and plan and deliver services accordingly. The strategy called on commissioners and service providers to specifically investigate:

> the means by which information might be obtained which will determine patterns of drug use and service needs, particularly where there are significant gaps in evidence, such as the needs of lesbian, gay, bisexual, transgender and transsexual (LGBT) people. (Home Office, 2008: 43)

The White Paper *Drug Strategy 2010: Reducing Demand, Restricting Supply, Building Recovery* (HMG, 2010b) was among the first initiatives introduced in November 2010 by the new government in England and Wales. Previous policies had recognised that some people may never be substance-free and the goal was to minimise harm and reduce the amount of substances consumed. The current approach signals a shift to recovery (which might mean total abstinence). It identifies key objectives of relevance for social workers including: support for the first years of life through the Healthy Child Programme; a commitment to the best start in life, which will see the recruitment of 4,200 health visitors; an enhancement of the Talk to Frank (the free confidential helpline) education and information service; early intervention for young people and families; and intensive support for young people. LGBT people are identified as a group in need of responsive services. Although this explicit commitment is welcomed, a report by the UK Drug Policy Commission (UKDPC) found that drug services have little relevance to Britain's diverse communities including LGBT communities (Beddoes et al, 2010). Better understanding of drug use within diverse communities could identify new or emergent patterns of drug use, and appropriate data-gathering mechanisms are needed to flag up potential health risks.

Relevance for social workers

Social workers may be ill-equipped to work with substance misuse as it is a topic that has been overlooked in social work training; they may believe, for example, that drug misuse is more serious than alcohol misuse, partly because drugs are illegal substances (Forrester and Harwin, 2006). Social workers need to understand the nature and extent of substance misuse and to recognise the signs of misuse in their work with service users. They may provide services directly for and with people with substance misuse problems in drug and alcohol services where the key issue is the substance misuse. In addition, they may provide support to families with children under the age of 16 where drug problems form one of a range of issues the family are experiencing, including those of parenting, relationships, financial issues, housing, risks of offending, physical and mental health, or problems relating to anger management.

Treatment services for substance misusers

The National Treatment Agency (NTA) updated its framework, *Models of Care*, for commissioning drug treatment in 2006 with a focus on integrating harm reduction interventions. Services for drug and alcohol misusers are organised into a four-tiered service intended to provide the same level of services in England. Tier 1 consists of a range of drug-related interventions that can be provided by generic services (in healthcare settings, including Accident and Emergency departments, and social care) depending on the competence of the practitioner and the partnership arrangements with specialised drug services where the main focus is not drug treatment (NTA, 2006). Social workers need to be aware of the Drug and Alcohol National Occupational Standards (DANOS), in particular, recognising indications of substance misuse, assessing risk and carrying out referral assessments. Tier 2 interventions include provision of information and advice, brief psychosocial interventions, harm reduction interventions (including needle exchange), complementary therapies, and support that does not form part of a care plan. These services have a low access threshold and include self-referrals. Tier 3 services include the provision of community-based specialist drug assessment and coordinated care planned treatment (NTA, 2006). Tier 4 interventions cater for people with a high level of need in drug and alcohol residential rehabilitation units, halfway houses or semi-supported residential care and can provide detoxification or assisted withdrawal services.

Practice models in work with substance misusers

Social workers are most likely to work alongside people whose behaviour causes the most harm to others – to their families or their communities – and the drug strategy explicitly links family support to anti-social behaviour. By the time a social worker has involvement with a service user, they may have been trying to stop or reduce their substance use over a number of years: a common pattern is a period of abstinence or reduced consumption followed by a relapse where the user returns to previous high consumption levels. Knowing about these behaviours enables social workers to become more effective in their interventions. Practice models can help social workers to understand that a relapse is not a slip or a so-called falling off the wagon; moreover, ambivalence, minimisation and resistance are characteristics in the cycle of change. While the service user may not see the impact that their dependency has on their partners and family, it may be that those close to them talk about wanting change. Good social work practice means that the rights of the family will be balanced with the needs of the individual. Social work values of autonomy and empowerment can play a key role in bringing about positive change in service users' behaviour and lifestyles.

Motivational interviewing: a practice model for substance misuse

Motivational interviewing is an approach that was developed through work in treating problem drinkers (Goodman, 2009). It is a useful model for social workers because it draws on principles of empowerment and working in partnership with service users. The social worker seeks to emphasise personal choice and the motivation for change is the responsibility of the service user. There are five principles which underpin the approach (see Goodman, 2009: 107–8):

1. Express empathy
    - Acceptance is a prerequisite to starting the process of change.
    - Reflective listening is an essential response.
    - Expect to be met with ambivalence.
    - The service user should be seen as capable of changing.

2. Develop discrepancy (between current lifestyle and future goals)
    - Awareness of consequences of no change is important.
    - The social worker needs to be directive.
    - A discrepancy between present behaviour and future goals will motivate change.
    - The service user should put forward the arguments for change.
3. Avoid argument
    - Arguments are counterproductive.
    - Defending breeds defensiveness.
    - Labelling is unnecessary.
4. Roll with resistance (if one technique is not working, try other strategies)
    - Momentum can be used to good advantage.
    - Involve the service user actively in problem solving.
5. Support self-efficacy
    - The service user will be motivated if they have a belief in the possibility of change.
    - The service user is responsible for choosing how they will change.
    - The social worker needs to believe in the user's ability to change.

The goal in motivational interviewing is to encourage a service user to change. Effective social work practice with substance misusers involves core social work values that avoid labelling; good interpersonal skills are needed alongside the ability to work dynamically with changing circumstances and knowledge of the possible stages a user may go through.

Underpinning knowledge

Substance misuse in LGBT communities

Concerns have been expressed about the nature and extent of substance misuse in LGBT communities over the past 20 years. Studies have suggested that the rates of use are higher in comparison to the general population. Possible explanations for this have included discrimination (McCabe et al, 2010), minority stress (Baiocco et al, 2010) and living in urban environments or in households with no children (Hoare, 2010). An individual's sense of connectedness to LGBT communities has also been associated with drug and alcohol misuse. Participants in a London study described being in a social network where alcohol and drug use were common and peer pressure to use drugs was high (Keogh et al, 2006). A large UK-wide study of gay and bisexual men identified factors associated with drug and alcohol use, such as mitigating social unease, alleviating loneliness or unhappiness, and enabling sexual encounters (Keogh et al, 2009).

Although poly-drug use is less common among BME gay and bisexual men in comparison to their white counterparts, a recent study revealed high levels of use (Halkitis and Jerome, 2008). The US study found that BME users did not live in neighbourhoods traditionally associated with LGBT communities and were more likely to be HIV-positive.

Among young LGBT people, substance misuse has been associated with the process of identity formation. In the first stages of coming out, the use of marijuana and alcohol increased as they became involved in LGBT-related activities. But once they had established a network of friends and support, their use of substances declined (Rosario et al, 2004b). Suicidal thoughts significantly increased the risk of drug use among young people while a positive reaction to the disclosure of sexual orientation served as a protective factor (Padilla et al, 2010). The authors argue that the role of strong family relationships in promoting young people's healthy development has implications for social work practice.

Knowledge about the nature and prevalence of substance misuse in the general population is derived from the British Crime Survey, which is a household survey conducted annually in England and Wales. The survey, which typically involves as many as 50,000 respondents, has provided key data to inform government policy over a period of 25 years. But it was not until 2007 that a question was included that asked respondents about their sexual orientation. The survey provides some initial population-based data about patterns of drug use in LGBT communities for the first time.

Illicit drug use reported in the British Crime Survey

The Home Office has undertaken an analysis of two-year combined data sets of the British Crime Survey, which yielded a sample of 985 LGBT people (Hoare, 2010). Findings reveal that they were three times more likely to have taken illicit drugs than heterosexual respondents. In the 12 months prior to the survey, they were more likely to report taking a Class A drug. Furthermore, they were five times more likely than the general population to use stimulant drugs such as cocaine, ecstasy, amphetamines and amyl nitrate.

Drug use is more common among younger people: it may be that the higher rates of drug use can be explained by the younger age profile of the LGBT respondents in the British Crime Survey. However, even after taking account of the age differences in the study, LGBT people continued to show elevated rates of use. Comparisons on the basis of gender showed that 38% of gay and bisexual men were last-year drug users compared with 13% of heterosexual men while 27% of lesbian and bisexual women used drugs in the preceding year compared with 7% of heterosexual women. Overall, drug prevalence is twice as high among men when compared to women in the general population; they had higher levels of use of all drug types. By contrast, among gay/bisexual men and lesbian/bisexual women there was more similarity in drug use (Hoare, 2010).

Prevalence of drug use among gay and bisexual men

In a study of gay and bisexual men, use of illicit drugs was found to be fairly common, with half having used at least one drug in the last year (Keogh et al, 2009). The three most commonly used drugs (both ever taken and taken in the last year) were alcohol, amyl nitrite and cannabis. However, these three drugs were also least likely to cause concern in their users. Few men used one substance only, excepting alcohol.

Perceptions of alcohol use

Historically, the only social space where it was safe for LGBT people to openly meet others was in venues known as the 'gay' scene. Socialising in bars and clubs may have contributed to increased alcohol consumption through simple exposure to alcohol or by alcohol giving the confidence needed to access the scene. Some explanations for problematic drinking suggest that cultural norms in LGBT communities encourage the consumption of alcohol. Increased use of alcohol has also been identified as a coping mechanism for dealing with discrimination: one study found that lesbians were more likely to use alcohol to reduce the effects of workplace harassment than gay men or heterosexual women (Nawyn et al, 2000). While social spaces available to LGBT people are no longer wholly concentrated in bars, these spaces are possibly still the most accessible and may be associated with binge drinking among younger bisexual and gay men (Eisenberg and Wechsler, 2008). Beliefs that lesbians and gay men have increased rates of problem drinking are pervasive among LGBT communities themselves. Even in a study that found comparable rates of drinking between lesbians and heterosexual women, the lesbians in the study were still more likely to believe that lesbians use alcohol excessively (Welch et al, 1998).

Patterns of alcohol consumption

The greatest difference in alcohol use patterns appears to be clustered among women in the 26- to 35-year-old age range. In comparison to heterosexual young women, lesbian and bisexual women are more likely to have used alcohol in the past month, more likely to have episodes of binge drinking in the past year and they report a higher average number of alcoholic drinks usually consumed when drinking (Ziyadeh et al, 2007). Among adult lesbian and bisexual women, abstention rates from alcohol are lower, they are more likely to be heavy drinkers and they are more likely to report alcohol-related social consequences, alcohol dependence and past help-seeking for an alcohol problem (Gruskin et al, 2001). By contrast, one study suggested that there are no differences in drinking levels between lesbians and heterosexual women and that heavy drinking or drinking-related problems have declined in recent years (Hughes and Jacobson, 2003). An analysis of the US national alcohol survey found that while gay and bisexual men spend comparatively more time in heavy drinking environments than do their heterosexual counterparts, they are not more likely to consume more alcohol.

Drug and alcohol treatment and prevention services

Some evidence suggests that LGBT people may experience greater barriers to accessing drug and alcohol treatment services because of the attitudes of treatment providers and the lack of culturally competent practice in service provision (Cochran and Cauce, 2006). There are conflicting findings about whether problematic drug and alcohol use is more prevalent in LGBT communities: Buffin and Mirza's (2009) study in Nottinghamshire suggested that the figures did not indicate greater cause for concern within the LGBT communities than for the population as a whole. By contrast, findings from the US suggest that LGBT people may have more severe substance misuse problems when entering treatment programmes than do heterosexual clients (Cochran and Cauce, 2006). There is some evidence to suggest that LGBT people may have different patterns of substance use, such as using drugs in a club environment, combination drug taking where users report taking two or more drugs at the same time, or mixing a number of drugs together with alcohol (Halkitis et al, 2007; Buffin and Mirza, 2009). Poly-drug use increases the possibility of mental or physical health problems and many drug fatalities result from poly-drug use. In addition, LGBT substance users may use a wider range of illicit drugs (Hoare, 2010) or use club drugs such as GHB (gamma-hydroxybutyrate) that are not recorded in the British Crime Survey (Browne et al, 2009).

Despite different patterns of substance misuse, there is a lack of evidence about good practice in drug treatment and prevention for LGBT service users; moreover, no studies have measured outcomes or evaluated service use (Beddoes et al, 2010). Small-scale studies have collected data from people accessing services on a self-referral basis and have asked participants about their satisfaction with or need for drug treatment and prevention services (Noret and Rivers, 2003; Jefferson and Tkaczuk, 2005; Browne et al, 2009). Factors that would help LGBT communities to access drug prevention services include building trust and demonstrating acceptance of sexual diversity. Some studies have found that problematic drug use is not self-assessed among LGBT research participants as being sufficiently serious to warrant professional support (Jefferson and Tkaczuk, 2005; Keogh et al, 2009). Making LGBT people aware of drug and alcohol services is a priority as many do not know about provision in their locality (Noret and Rivers, 2003).

Studies have tended to focus on the substance-using behaviours of MSM (men who have sex with men) and, in particular, concerns about the transmission of HIV and the potential increased risk (Jefferson and Tkaczuk, 2005). For gay and bisexual men, problematic alcohol or drug use may arise through a culture of acceptance and be associated with the specificities of gay men's intimate and social lives (Keogh et al, 2009). Other groups are less likely to have been included in research samples; few UK studies have specifically considered substance misuse among lesbian and bisexual women and trans people have been particularly overlooked (Buffin and Mirza, 2009).

Conclusion

Keogh et al (2009) argue that access routes to treatment, which are largely through the criminal justice system, may mean that gay and bisexual men are less likely to come into contact with drug treatment services and this may disadvantage them. Substance misuse services should routinely monitor service uptake by LGBT people and produce data about the outcome of treatment interventions.

Key questions in substance misuse social work with LGBT people

- ➲ How do LGBT people access information and services relating to alcohol and drug misuse in your local community?
- ➲ What are the risk factors for LGBT people that may increase susceptibility to alcohol and drug misuse?
- ➲ Identify effective interventions and treatment programmes in alcohol or drug misuse with LGBT communities.

Further reading

Buffin, J. and Mirza, I. (2009) *Outing Notts: A Study into the Substance Misuse Needs and Experiences of LGBT People across Nottinghamshire,* University of Central Lancashire with Safer Nottingham Drug and Alcohol Team.

Browne, K., McGlynn, N. and Lim, J. (2009) *Drugs and Alcohol – Additional Findings Report: Count Me In Too: LGBT Lives in Brighton and Hove,* Brighton: Spectrum.

Department of Health and Human Services (2001) *A Provider's Introduction to Substance Abuse Treatment for Lesbian, Gay, Bisexual, and Transgender Individuals.* Washington, DC: Department of Health and Human Services.

Gold, D. and Cowan, K. (2009) 'Mapping LGBT Westminster: investigating the needs and experiences of LGBT people in Westminster', Westminster City Council. Available at: https://www.westminster.gov.uk/workspace/assets/publications/Mapping-LGBT-Westminster-FINAL-1245247095.pdf

Hoare, J. (2010) 'Annex 2: nationally representative estimates of illicit drug use by self-reported sexual orientation, 2006/07–2008/09 BCS', in Hoare, J. and Moon, D. (eds) *Drug Misuse Declared: Findings from the 2009/10 British Crime Survey, Home Office Statistical Bulletin 13/10,* London: Home Office. Available at: http://www.homeoffice.gov.uk/rds/pdfs10/hosb1310.pdf

Jefferson, G. and Tkaczuk, N. (2005) *Outing Drugs: Report of the Community-Led Research Project Focusing on Drug and Alcohol Use by Gay Men's Health Wiltshire and Swindon amongst the Gay and Bisexual Male Communities in Wiltshire and Swindon,* Swindon: Gay Men's Health.

Keogh, P., Reid, D., Bourne, A., Weatherburn, P., Hickson, F., Jessup, K. and Hammond, G. (2009) *Wasted Opportunities: Problematic Alcohol and Drug Use among Gay Men and Bisexual Men,* London: Sigma Research.

Noret, N. and Rivers, I. (2003) 'Drug and alcohol use among LGBTs in the City of Leeds', Social Inclusion & Diversity Research into Practice, York, St John College.

PATH (Partnership Action on Tobacco and Health) (2010) *Stop-Smoking Service Provision for LGBT Communities in Scotland. Edinburgh: PATH.*

UKDPC (UK Drug Policy Commission) (2010) 'Drugs and diversity: lesbian, gay, bisexual and transgender (LGBT) communities: learning from the evidence'. Available at: www.ukdpc.org.uk/reports/shtml

Varney, J. (2008) 'A review of drugs and alcohol use amongst the lesbian, gay, bisexual and transgender community in London', London: LGBT Advisory Group.

Wilde, B. (2009) *Sorted Out: Bristol Lesbian, Gay, Bisexual and Trans Drug & Alcohol Survey.* Bristol: Safer Bristol, Crime and Drugs Partnership.

Asylum seekers and refugees

Practice scenario

I went to Croydon, queued up and got a ticket. That was the most daunting thing. This place has no privacy. I was called to a window. The guy next door could hear what I was saying and so could the guys behind me. You're talking behind Perspex. The thing I found so difficult was, as a gay man coming from a country where you don't talk about sex, the first contact I had, the interviewer was an elderly Asian lady, someone I'd put in a place like my mum. She asked: why are you seeking asylum? It was the hardest thing to tell her. I kept saying because I like men. She said: what do you mean? It was very tough to explain that I'm gay. It's like she didn't understand – like she thought what I was talking about is vile and horrible. It was so uncomfortable. She asked me: why have you taken five months before coming? I said I didn't know this existed.... In a few minutes some guys came ... they searched me and kept me for six hours in this small room. People kept coming in crying. That's when my world started changing. (Robert, Ugandan asylum-seeker, in Miles, 2010: 11)

Questions

This chapter identifies some of the issues for Robert in seeking asylum in the UK as a gay man. Consider the following questions as you read the chapter to inform your practice in social work with LGBT asylum seekers:

➲ Why does Robert need to come out in order to claim asylum?
➲ Are there any personal, cultural or institutional barriers for him in disclosing his sexual orientation?
➲ In what ways do LGBT people have unequal protections worldwide?

Introduction

The international setting provides an important context for LGBT people's rights in the UK because many of the rights they enjoy have come about because of judgments made in the European Court of Human Rights or through human rights advances globally for LGBT people (de Jong, 2003). Since 2007, the International Lesbian and Gay Association (ILGA), a campaigning organisation for LGBT people's rights worldwide, has published an annual report – *State Sponsored Homophobia* – which identifies the international legal situation for LGBT people. The struggle for social equality has gained momentum by the collaboration of advocates from diverse countries globally and not only those in Western nations. A group of experts met in Yogyakarta, Indonesia in 2007 to draw up a universal guide to human rights and sexual orientation and gender identity. The Yogyakarta Principles outline 29 fundamental freedoms including the right to found a family, the right to social protection measures and the right to seek asylum (International Service for Human Rights, 2007).

Unequal protections

Globally, there are unequal protections for LGBT people in United Nations (UN) member states despite the existence of a UN resolution which recognised that sexual orientation should be a status that is protected from discrimination. This resolution was recently overturned by a UN General Assembly meeting that voted to remove sexual orientation and gender identity from a resolution on extrajudicial, summary or arbitrary executions in 2010. Around the world, people face discrimination, violence, rape, imprisonment, torture or execution because of their actual or perceived sexual orientation or gender identity by the state or people acting on behalf of the state, from their own communities or their families (de Gruchy and Fish, 2004). In 76 UN member states, same-sex sexual behaviour between consenting adults is criminalised. Five countries impose the death penalty: Iran, Mauritania, Saudi Arabia, Sudan and Yemen (plus some parts of Nigeria and Somalia) (Ottosson, 2010); one of the most shocking examples was the public hanging of two gay Iranian teenagers in 2005, whose state execution was widely reported in the world media.

In 14 countries, men are imprisoned simply for being gay (Ottosson, 2010). In South Africa, despite constitutional protection, 30 lesbians have been brutally murdered over the past decade. Eudy Simelane, from the national female football squad, was raped and murdered because she lived openly as a lesbian; others are subjected to so-called corrective rape (Kelly, 2009).

Some jurisdictions have introduced new legislation to ban marriage between same-sex couples, most notably in California, where Proposition 8 stated that only heterosexual marriage is recognised as valid in the state; this judgment overturned a previous Supreme Court ruling that same-sex couples have a constitutional right to marry. The road to marriage equality has suffered a number of setbacks; the introduction in the US of the Defense of Marriage Act 1996 had effectively barred the legal recognition of LGBT relationships by provisions which state that marriage is a union between a man and a woman. In a similar vein, following the election pledge of President Clinton to lift the ban on LGBT people serving in the armed forces, the policy known as 'Don't Ask, Don't Tell' was introduced in 1993, which allowed LGBT people to serve as long as they kept their sexual orientation private.

Global rights for LGBT people

Human rights legislation has formed the lynchpin for the recognition of same-sex relationships (Fish, 2009b). In 1994, South Africa became the first country to include protection on the grounds of sexual orientation in its constitution and two years later it was one of the first countries to recognise same-sex civil unions: there are now 23 countries where same-sex relationships are legally recognised including Columbia, Peru, Brazil, Australia and New Zealand. In 2001, the Netherlands became the first country to legalise marriage for same-sex partners; other countries have since followed this lead including Belgium, Spain, Iceland, Argentina and Mexico. But the rights conferred by legal recognition differ between countries. In some countries, civil partnership confers more rights than afforded by same-sex marriage; however, there are continuing concerns that a two-tier system has been established with LGBT people afforded second-class status (King and Bartlett, 2006).

Anti-discrimination legislation has been introduced in 53 countries worldwide including countries in South America, Europe and Australasia (Ottosson 2010). Eight countries (Argentina, Belgium, Iceland, the Netherlands, Norway, Sweden, South Africa and Spain) afford full non-discrimination including marriage and adoption. On 2 July 2009, the High Court of Delhi ruled that the Indian penal code could no longer be applied to prohibit sexual activities between consenting same-sex adults.

LGBT human rights advocates have identified a number of rights and freedoms that are necessary for LGBT equality; the decriminalisation of consenting sexual relations between adults represents a core rights issue worldwide. Advocates have pressed for state recognition of same-sex relationships through civil unions or marriage, allowing LGBT people to serve openly in the armed forces, an equal age of consent, protection from discrimination in public services, allowing same-sex couples to jointly adopt, hate crime laws to protect LGBT people from harassment or violence, immigration equality, freedom of peaceful assembly (a number of Pride marches have been banned in Eastern Europe) and recognised status for asylum.

Recognition of LGBT as a protected status

For a number of years, sexual orientation and gender identity were not internationally recognised among the reasons for persecution for which people could claim refugee status (de Jong, 2003). Under Article 1, the 1951 United Nations Convention Relating to the Status of Refugees stated that grounds for protection should include one's social identity:

> A refugee is a person who owing to well-founded fear of being persecuted for reasons of race, religion, nationality, membership of a particular social group or political opinion, is outside the country of his nationality and is unable or, owing to such fear, is unwilling to avail himself [sic] of the protection of that country; or who not having a nationality and being outside the country of his former habitual residence as a result of such events, is unable or, owing to such fear, is unwilling to return to it.

The provisions of the Convention refer to 'membership of a particular social group' as a protected identity; in 1999, this was extended by a UK House of Lords decision to sexual orientation as grounds for protection and the judgment recognised that LGBT people constituted a group by whom claims could be made. The UN High Commissioner for Refugees (UNHCR, 2008) issued a guidance note calling on all UN member states to recognise sexual orientation and gender identity as Convention grounds for refugee status.

In order to claim asylum on the grounds of sexual orientation or gender identity, an asylum seeker needs to demonstrate that they have been subjected to physical, sexual or verbal abuse and discrimination. There is also a requirement to show that their government was unable or unwilling to offer them protection and to punish the perpetrators. LGBT people most commonly make a claim for asylum under the category of a particular social group and must show that:

- a particular social group exists;
- the applicant is a member of the particular social group;
- the applicant has a well-founded fear of persecution owing to such membership (see European Council on Refugees and Exiles (ELENA), 1997: 1)

Recognition of sexual orientation as a particular social group has been hampered by the lack of a coherent definition. There have been a number of judicial decisions relating to what constitutes membership of a particular social group that have led to defining factors (ELENA, 1997). In itself, membership of a particular social group is insufficient to substantiate a claim of refugee status. There must also be evidence that such membership is at 'the root of persecution … or the very existence of the group as such, is held to be an obstacle to the government's policies' (ELENA, 1997: 1).

Criminal sanctions or prevailing social and cultural norms may mean that many LGBT applicants have led hidden lives. In consequence, they may have little evidence to prove their identity as LGBT people because they were not living openly in their country of origin. There may be a social expectation to marry and have a family and some may be obliged to enter into a forced marriage. By refusing to marry, they may fear that they will be identified as LGBT by their communities (UNHCR, 2008). If they have been married they may find it very difficult to demonstrate their identity.

Issues for LGBT people seeking asylum in the UK

Higher refusal rates

There is evidence that lesbians and gay men face distinct barriers in having their asylum claims upheld. The UK Lesbian and Gay Immigration Group (UKLGIG) is the only dedicated support organisation in the UK for LGBT asylum seekers. Their research showed higher refusal rates for claims made on the basis of sexual orientation compared to those made on other grounds (98% versus 73%) (UKLGIG, 2010). The study, which reviewed Home Office Reason for Refusal letters (these only related to claims made by lesbians and gay men), found that decision-makers did not fully understand the issues and there were areas where existing guidance and legislation was not adhered to.

The initial screening interview

The procedure for claiming asylum involves attending an asylum-screening interview at the port of entry or at the screening unit in Croydon, London as soon as possible after arrival in the UK. Although the purpose of this initial interview is to establish the person's identity and their country of origin, the final question asks the applicant for their reasons for claiming asylum (Miles, 2010). The screening interview, as in the practice scenario above, takes place in a public environment that is not conducive to the disclosure of sexual orientation. If, at this stage, the applicant fails to mention sexual orientation as a ground for their claim, they may receive a poor rating, which might impact on the assessment of their credibility. A negative assessment is a significant factor in refusals: 'It's held against you, not disclosing at the earliest opportunity: Come on, you're in a safe country, why didn't you disclose it as soon as you came into contact?' (Jody, UK Border Agency [UKBA] presenting officer, in Miles, 2010: 10).

Almost half of all claims were refused because the applicant was not believed to be a lesbian or a gay man (UKLGIG, 2010). Sexual orientation is multifaceted and may be based on one or more of the following domains: behaviour (expressed by who they have sexual relations with), desire (expressed in who they are attracted to) or identity (expressed by how they feel about themselves). Typically, most Home Office *case owners* (the UKBA official who has oversight of the claim) assume that sexual orientation is defined solely by sexual behaviour and if an applicant does not describe same-sexual relations the credibility of their claim is questioned:

> They asked about who you have sex with, how many people you have sex with and how many times. I still feel scared to talk about it. When you come from a country where you've never told anyone and now you have five people asking you questions about this – I found it difficult to talk about. (Nigerian asylum-seeker, in Miles, 2010: 17)

This emphasis on sexual behaviour ignores the fact that an applicant may never have told someone else that they are LGBT and it is even less likely that they will have talked about same-sex relationships with anyone previously. Moreover, in many countries, there are no terms for lesbian or gay; how then does one begin to talk about feeling attracted to someone of the same sex when the words do not exist in the language? Many LGBT people live partially closeted lives to avoid social sanctions in their country of origin: 'Back home you live in a box, you're locked away. You learn to be invisible. You have to deny who you are, and what you want. It's like you're leading a double life, it's Jekyll and Hyde' (Jamaican asylum seeker, in Miles, 2010: 12).

Not having told someone about your sexual orientation is sufficient reason for case owners to disbelieve the claim (UKLGIG, 2009). Because of these circumstances, there is usually no documentary evidence by which to prove the person's sexual orientation (ELENA, 1997). For this reason, some refugee support organisations advise their service users to socialise in LGBT bars and clubs so that they are seen in LGBT venues. In Bell and Hansen's (2009) study, frequenting the LGBT commercial scene was seen as a means of establishing sexual orientation and providing evidence in legal proceedings. But there are barriers to participating on the 'scene', which include the financial costs of entry to and drinking in such venues. Some participants in the *Over Not Out* study (Bell and Hansen, 2009) experienced sexual exploitation and racial discrimination and, for some, the scene was not considered to be a place where meaningful relationships could be formed, while others were able meet people there to develop social networks.

Applicants are more likely to be refused if they do not look gay; this includes stereotyped notions that gay men are effeminate or flamboyant and lesbians are masculine and childless. These assumptions ignore the social pressures to keep identities or behaviour hidden. Heller (2009) deploys the concepts of 'covering' (ie passing as heterosexual) and 'reverse covering' (ie adopting an overt identity in order to be accepted as an LGBT person) to articulate these two demands. She argues that marginalised groups are obliged to cover aspects of their identity so that they can access the social and political benefits available to the majority. Understanding these expectations will support social workers in negotiating the complexity of the asylum process and in recognising that these twin demands represent a serious form of oppression:

> Being compelled to forsake or conceal one's sexual orientation and gender identity, where this is instigated or condoned by the State, may amount to persecution. LGBT persons who live in fear of being publicly identified will often conceal their sexual orientation as a result in order to avoid the severe consequences of such exposure, including the risk of incurring harsh criminal penalties, arbitrary house raids, dismissal from employment and societal disapproval. Such actions can not only be considered discriminatory and as violating the right to privacy, but also as infringing the right to freedom of opinion and expression. (UNHCR, 2008: 8)

It is assumed that because someone may have lived in a clandestine manner before they made the decision to flee their country of origin, they can return to their country of origin and relocate to a different region and thus evade persecution. In making the decision about whether it is safe for someone to return, case owners consider whether the applicant could keep their sexual orientation hidden. This expectation was known as the 'discretion requirement' and means that an asylum claim could be refused if it is believed that the applicant could return to their country and behave discreetly (UKLGIG, 2010: 4). Home Office case owners· believed that behaving discreetly simply meant that people should not have sex in public or in places where they might be discovered. But a secret and clandestine life in their home country meant that many LGBT people were not able to 'meet a potential partner, live with a partner, socialise or express their identity in any public way without fear of grave harm' (UKLGIG, 2009: 4). In 2010, a UK Supreme Court ruling in the case of two gay men overturned the discretion requirement, Lord Hope said: 'To compel a homosexual person to pretend that his [sic] sexuality does not exist or suppress the behaviour by which to manifest itself is to deny his fundamental right to be who he is.' (Lord Hope, 7 July 2010, reading the Supreme Court ruling on 'HT' [Cameroon] and 'J' [Iran]).

The requirement ignored the realities of people's lives; in a number of countries, LGBT people hide from fear of persecution rather than from a choice to remain hidden. The 'discretion' requirement that obliged someone to conceal their sexual orientation stood in contradiction to the category of a particular social group as one of the protected grounds in the 1951 Convention (UNHCR, 2008).

Jill Power, for the UKLGIG, says that while LGBT applicants who are refused asylum have a right to appeal to an immigration court, courts represent a difficult environment in which to contest deportation: 'Court hearings are a nerve racking and frightening experience for our clients. They feel anxious, exposed and afraid because the most private aspect of their life is put on trial' (UKLGIG, 2009).

Asylum is granted on the basis of whether the applicant has a well-founded fear of persecution; this decision is informed by Country of Origin Information Reports, which provide data relating to LGBT issues on legislation, social attitudes and treatment (Bell and Hansen, 2009). There are sometimes discrepancies between the Home Office perspective of the relative safety of a country and the accounts of people seeking asylum from those countries. In some countries, there is no legislation that prohibits same-sex relationships; rather, people face prosecution under public decency laws. The quality of the information available to the Home Office may be limited, 'particularly for countries where LGBT persons may feel obliged to conduct their personal lives in a clandestine manner' (Bell and Hansen, 2009: 67).

Current UK policy commitments to LGBT asylum seekers

The *Programme for Government* (HMG, 2010c) of the new Coalition makes a clear commitment to building a fairer society by removing barriers to social mobility. The strategy outlines seven actions in relation to equalities issues and makes explicit pledges to protect LGBT asylum seekers and to promote global rights:

- We will stop the deportation of asylum seekers who have had to leave particular countries because their sexual orientation or gender identification puts them at proven risk of imprisonment, torture or execution.

- We will use our relationships with other countries to push for unequivocal support for gay rights and for UK civil partnerships to be recognised internationally. (HMG, 2010c: 18)

Research with LGBT asylum seekers

A study conducted by Refugee Support – *Over Not Out* – interviewed 40 LGBT asylum seekers from 15 countries about their experiences of housing and homelessness (Bell and Hansen, 2009: 67). It revealed multiple disadvantages in housing, health, asylum support services and social isolation. Harassment from landlords led them to be fearful of their safety:

> I have had problems with the landlord. He would not give me peace. He knew I was an asylum seeker and he would open my mail. He kicked me out because I was gay. The landlord never liked me. (Armenian gay man, 25–29 years old, in Bell and Hansen, 2009: 18)

Key findings from the study included (Bell and Hansen, 2009: 38, 50):

- LGBT asylum seekers are exceptionally transient, often experiencing 'hidden homelessness' as they stay for short and indeterminate periods in the homes of friends and acquaintances.
- Most have experienced multiple forms of anti-LGBT discrimination, harassment and abuse and many fear disclosing their sexuality or gender identity and live 'double lives'.
- LGBT asylum seekers, especially in areas of dispersal, feel unsafe in the surrounding area and suffer anti-LGBT harassment from neighbours and local people.
- Gay men are particularly vulnerable to sexual exploitation as asylum seekers; some lesbian asylum seekers have experienced attempted rape in UK Border Agency and shared accommodation.
- LGBT asylum seekers can face insecurity from slander and blackmail, in some cases losing sources of income or housing, when their sexuality or gender identity is exposed.
- Many LGBT asylum seekers are especially mistrustful of the police and reluctant to report abuse. For some this is due to the experience of abuse or torture by authorities in their country of origin specifically because of their sexuality or gender identity.
- Many LGBT asylum seekers have lost family support due to their sexuality or gender identity.
- They cannot rely on their respective national or ethnic communities for support because they fear anti-LGBT reprisals from them.

■ LGBT and BME organisations fulfil vital service provision and support functions for LGBT asylum seekers that are not available from other refugee support organisations and refugee community organisations.

Trans asylum seekers

Human rights abuses

The UNHCR (2008) guidance note recognised that gender identity forms a particular social group and that trans people face distinct issues when applying for asylum:

> These could, for example, relate to accessing health care or due to an increased risk of exposure to harm if their gender identity is not legally recognized (where, for instance, they are not able to change their name and sex in the civil registry). Such exposure could, for instance, be prompted where a transgender individual is asked by the authorities to produce identity documents and his or her physical appearance does not correspond to the sex as indicated in the documents. (UNHCR, 2008: 9)

While some jurisdictions have recognised that lesbians and gay men constitute a particular social group, estimates suggest that in 1996 there were 7,000 claims for asylum on these grounds worldwide (ELENA, 1997). By contrast, claims relating to bisexual and trans people are less common or go unrecorded.

Amnesty International has documented cases for a number of years to highlight the discrimination experienced by trans people. Their report revealed that in some countries in the Americas, trans people experienced high levels of discrimination and abuse. They suffered torture and ill-treatment for transgressing gender boundaries and changing the sex they were assigned at birth:

> Vanessa Lorena Ledesma, a trans woman, was arrested in Córdoba, Argentina, on 11 February 2000 during a scuffle at a bar. Five days later she was dead. A police report recorded that she had died as a result of a 'cardiac arrest'. However, an autopsy reportedly revealed that her body showed signs of torture, including severe bruising. (Amnesty International, 2001: 16)

In some provinces in Argentina, the police were able to detain people for cross–dressing under offences against public decency (Amnesty International,

2001). The report found evidence that trans people were often attacked in ways that sought to undermine their bodily identities, for example, by being beaten on their cheekbones or breasts in order to burst their implants and cause psychological as well as physical harm (Amnesty International, 2001). A report to the United Nations Human Rights Committee documented human rights abuses during the period 2004–10 of trans people in El Salvador (IGLHRC, 2010). Many of the experiences were not published in the media, nor were they reported by the victims' families to the police.

Legal protections

The Directorate-General for Internal Policies of the European Parliament produced guidance on trans people's rights in 27 EU member states (Castagnoli, 2010). In some countries, trans people are protected from discrimination on the basis of sex discrimination laws, in others under sexual orientation legislation, while other countries have no legislation. The report provides details about the requirements for gender reassignment (eg hormonal treatment and/or surgery), the legal position regarding changing names, the availability of changing the birth certificate, the possibility of marriage in the new gender and the obligation to obtain a divorce before marriage in the new gender. In comparison to the lesbian, gay and bisexual rights movement, trans activism is a more recent development in many countries.

Trans people's experiences of seeking asylum in the UK

There are, then, comparatively few recent studies that have investigated human rights abuses against trans people or their experiences of seeking asylum. One London study estimated that between 20 and 30 people each year enter the UK to seek asylum on the basis of gender identity (Bell and Hansen, 2009). Bell and Hansen's (2009) study investigated the specific issues experienced by trans people seeking asylum. Several people in their study had been held in a UK detention centre and described adverse experiences. While such experiences are commonly reported by all those who are detained, the report indicated that these experiences were intensified by homophobia and transphobia from other detainees and staff. Professionals showed a lack of sensitivity in providing for the needs of trans detainees, often placing them in cells with people from the same ethnic or cultural background who showed hostility to them because of their gender identity. In another account, a trans man relates the difficulties he encountered in being held in a female detention centre:

> Four-and-a-half months. And female detention centre. Everybody there asking me, 'How you having sex with your girlfriend?' Even immigration officer asking me, 'What are you, male or female?' I say, 'What do you mean?' Whole world asking me this question so now I am confused. So I say, 'Female.' He say, 'No, I am confused. So I send you in medical examination.' The immigration officer asked me, 'Are you comfortable with female or male doctor.' I said female doctor. He said, 'If we don't have female doctor what do we do? You go to the male doctor.' This is immigration officer, a Home Office person. (Trans man, in Bell and Hansen, 2009: 24–5)

Many LGBT asylum seekers chose to live in London and refused UKBA accommodation despite the fact that this decision had made them destitute. The absence of family support means that trans people in particular may rely on social networks for support and the expertise that lawyers have developed in supporting asylum applications for trans people. London also offers a larger pool of dedicated voluntary-sector organisations not found in other towns and cities in the UK:

> How can I go Midlands because I don't know anything about Midlands? No friends, if I want to come to UKLGIG meeting or Female-to-Male meeting every week or every month, or any other organisation. There are many organisations in London. How can I attend this meeting? (Trans man, in Bell and Hansen, 2009: 26)

Social work with asylum seekers

Local authorities have a duty to assess all individuals (including failed asylum seekers); social workers may undertake a community care assessment under section 47 of the NHS and Community Care Act 1990. They also have a duty to provide care under section 21 of the National Assistance Act 1948. The Slough judgment (House of Lords, 2008) ruled that in order to qualify for support, an individual must have a care need above the provision of accommodation. Schedule 3 of the Nationality, Immigration and Asylum Act 2002 prevents local authorities from providing support to refused asylum seekers who have remained in the country unlawfully; however, the Human Rights Act 1998 allows local authorities to provide assistance if to do otherwise would be in breach of the person's human rights (Newbigging et al, 2010).

Asylum seekers form a marginalised group and may experience inequalities in their access to health and social care due to the bureaucracy of service provision, resource constraints, language, cultural differences and racism (Hill et al, 2009). Weaver and Burns (2001: 160–1) identify a number of implications for social work practice, including:

- Be aware that asylum seekers … who have not yet obtained legal permission to resettle … may be suspicious of helping professionals and reluctant to disclose much information;
- Work to establish a trusting relationship with your client and refer him/her to the appropriate agency that provides immigration and legal representation;
- Develop a working knowledge of local and national resources for refugees and asylum seekers;
- Create a safe environment that will enable a refugee to feel comfortable discussing trauma and/or torture. This includes recognition that both asylum seekers and helping professionals may view these as taboo subjects;
- Do not probe or push a refugee to disclose information about trauma. Rather let the client know that many asylum seekers have experienced trauma and you are willing to talk about it, if this would be helpful;
- Working with asylum seekers puts social workers at risk for burnout and vicarious traumatisation. It is important for a social worker to recognize his or her own need for professional wellness and take steps to take care of him or herself after hearing stories of trauma and torture.

Social work students may work alongside asylum seekers on placement in a voluntary agency that offers specialised support services. Social workers may take a number of roles with this service user group, including advocating for individuals, supporting people to make claims, helping them to resettle in the UK and supporting their recovery from trauma (Weaver and Burns, 2001; Newbigging et al, 2010).

Conclusion

There has been relatively little discussion about the needs of LGBT asylum seekers in the UK social work literature (see Newbigging et al, 2010). There is a need for social workers to understand the ways in which the process of seeking asylum is distinctive for LGBT people; for example, knowing about the requirements for the credibility of a claim, the recent ruling on discretion and the lack of state protection for LGBT people in many countries throughout the world. LGBT people may have unique experiences as they wait for the decision about their claim. Research suggests that UKBA accommodation may not be suitable for LGBT asylum seekers because of 'intolerable levels of homophobia and the failure of landlords to tackle this' (Bell and Hansen, 209: 68). Bell and Hansen's (2009) study also found that LGBT asylum seekers who were dispersed to other cities moved to London to reduce social isolation by being closer to friends and LGBT community resources. Rights-based approaches are fundamental to good practice alongside the ability to challenge common stereotypes in the media about so-called bogus claimants and skills to work effectively in a crisis.

Key questions for social workers with LGBT asylum seekers

➲   What is the international legal basis for LGBT claims for asylum?

➲   Compare the rights and freedoms achieved by LGBT people in Western and Eastern Europe.

➲   What are some of the challenges for social workers with LGBT asylum seekers?

➲   Find out about local and national agencies and resources to support your practice with LGBT asylum seekers.

Resources

LGBT Asylum News is a campaigning group that was set up to prevent the deportation of a young Iranian gay man. It provides information about the countries of origin and the personal stories of LGBT asylum seekers. Their website is available at: http://madikazemi.blogspot.com/p/asylum-stories.html

International legislation relating to asylum

1948 Universal Declaration of Human Rights
1951 United Nations Convention Relating to the Status of Refugees
1966 International Covenant on Civil and Political Rights
1967 Protocol Relating to the Status of Refugees

UK legislation

■ **National Assistance Act 1948** – Section 21 places a duty on local authorities to provide support. (Where an applicant is a failed asylum seeker and they have no need other than for accommodation and support to meet essential living needs, there is no duty on local authorities to support under section 21.)

- **Immigration and Asylum Act 1999** – This legislation introduced the dispersal of asylum seekers from London and the South East to other parts of the UK. Section 4 provides refused asylum seekers with short-term support in the form of accommodation and vouchers, while waiting to return to their home country.
- **Nationality, Immigration and Asylum Act 2002** – Section 55 states that a claim for asylum must be made within a reasonable period (which is often defined as 24 hours).
- **Asylum and Immigration (Treatment of Claimants, etc) Act 2004** – especially section 8 regarding claimant's credibility.
- **Immigration, Asylum and Nationality Act 2006**
- **Borders, Citizenship and Immigration Act 2009** – Section 55 states that the UK Border Agency must have arrangements in place to safeguard and promote the welfare of children in discharging its functions.

International organisations

- **Asylum Law** – Asylum Law was founded in 1999 with the purpose of using the internet to help legal representatives to prepare asylum cases. It has dedicated pages for LGBT asylum. Its website is available at: http://www.asylumlaw.org
- **Amnesty International** – Amnesty International works to bring about a fair and effective asylum system. The organisation seeks to achieve this by carrying out research into aspects of asylum policy and practice, developing proposals for improving policy and practice, and promoting these proposals with government, members of parliament and other influential audiences. Its website is available at: http://www.amnesty.org.uk/index.asp
- **Human Rights Watch (HRW)** – HRW is one of the world's leading independent organisations dedicated to defending and protecting human rights. Their rigorous, objective investigations and strategic, targeted advocacy build intense pressure for action and raise the cost of human rights abuse. For 30 years, Human Rights Watch has worked tenaciously to lay the legal and moral groundwork for deep-rooted change and has fought to bring greater justice and security to people around the world. HRW has an LGBT programme that has undertaken work in Senegal, Iran, Cameroon, Russia and Egypt (De Gruchy and Fish, 2004). Its website is available at: http://www.hrw.org/en/home
- **International Gay and Lesbian Human Rights Commission (IGLHRC)** – IGLHRC is a leading international organisation dedicated to human rights advocacy on behalf of people who experience

discrimination or abuse on the basis of their actual or perceived sexual orientation, gender identity or expression. Its website is available at: http://www.iglhrc.org

- **International Lesbian, Gay, Bisexual, Trans and Intersex Association (ILGA)** – Since 1978, ILGA has been campaigning for LGBT and intersex rights. Its aim is to work for the equality of lesbian, gay, bisexual, trans and intersex people and their liberation from all forms of discrimination. ILGA produce an annual report of LGBT rights worldwide and their website features an interactive map of global rights and penalties. Its website is available at: http://ilga.org

UK organisations

- **Information Centre about Asylum and Refugees (ICAR)** – ICAR is an academic research and information organisation based at the Runnymede Trust. ICAR aims to encourage understanding, public debate and policymaking about asylum and refugees in the UK, grounded in accurate and academically sourced information. It produced a navigation guide (de Jong, 2003) for issues relevant to LGBT asylum seekers and refugees, which provided comprehensive information on UK case law. Its website is available at: http://www.icar.org.uk
- **Refugee Support** – Refugee Support is the specialist refugee and asylum seeker service provider for Metropolitan Support Trust (MST). It is a leading provider of housing and support for refugees and asylum seekers and operates across three regions: the Midlands, Yorkshire and London. MST commissioned *Over Not Out* (Bell and Hansen, 2009), the UK study of housing and homelessness among LGBT asylum seekers. Its website is available at: http://www.mst-online.org.uk/
- **Stonewall** – Stonewall is the largest lobbying group for LGBT people with bases in England, Scotland and Wales. Stonewall campaigns have included rights in the workplace, tackling homophobic bullying in schools, health and healthcare, crime, families and parenting, sport, the media, and immigration and asylum. Stonewall commissioned the study *No Going Back: Lesbian and Gay People and the Asylum System* (Miles, 2010), which included interviews with UKBA staff, legal professionals, asylum support workers and people seeking asylum. Its website is available at: http://www.stonewall.org.uk
- **UK Lesbian and Gay Immigration Group (UKLGIG)** – UKLGIG was set up to campaign for immigration rights for same-sex couples and increasingly assists LGBT people who have come to the UK to seek a safe haven from persecution. Its asylum-related activities include:

> *Support for LGBT Asylum Seekers:* providing support and information via a helpline and in person; referring to solicitors; organising a monthly support meeting; visiting detention centres; and running other social support projects.
> *Research and Policy:* monitoring and researching relevant (legal) developments and issues; researching human rights in countries of origin; working to ensure LGBT people are treated equally and with dignity in the asylum process; seeking to improve the quality of UKBA decision-making; and networking with organisations and individuals working on related issues in the UK and internationally. The report *Failing the Grade* (UKLGIG, 2010) reviewed Home Office initial decisions on lesbian and gay claims for asylum.
> *Training and Information:* providing training and information on LGBT asylum issues to relevant service providers in the refugee and LGBT community, solicitors and other legal advisers, UKBA staff and the judiciary.

Its website is available at: http://www.uklgig.org.uk

Further reading

Bell, M. and Hansen, C. (2009) *Over Not Out: The Housing and Homelessness Issues Specific to Lesbian, Gay, Bisexual and Transgender Asylum Seekers,* London: Refugee Support.

de Jong, J. (2003) *Lesbian, Gay, Bisexual and Transgender (LGBT) Refugees and Asylum Seekers,* London: Information Centre about Asylum and Refugees in the UK (ICAR).

Miles, N. (2010) *No Going Back: Lesbian and Gay People and the Asylum System,* London: Stonewall.

Newbigging, K., Thomas, N., Coupe, J., Habte-Mariam, Z., Ahmed, N., Shah, A. and Hicks, J. (2010) *Good Practice in Social Care with Refugees and Asylum Seekers,* London: Social Care Institute for Excellence.

UKLGIG (UK Lesbian and Gay Immigration Group) (2010) *Failing the Grade: Home Office Initial Decisions on Lesbian and Gay Claims for Asylum,.* London: UK Lesbian and Gay Immigration Group.

UNHCR (UN High Commissioner for Refugees) (2008) 'Guidance Note on Refugee Claims Relating to Sexual Orientation and Gender Identity'. Available at: http://www.unhcr.org/refworld/docid/48abd5660.html (accessed 3 December 2010).

Concluding remarks

This book is intended as a stage in the journey towards developing good practice in social work with LGBT people and to underpin learning on qualifying programmes in higher education. There are some gaps and limitations in the book. Although there are a number of voluntary-sector organisations who work with BME communities, indicating distinctive concerns, studies with and for LGBT people from BME communities are notably absent in research in social work and related disciplines. For this reason, separate consideration has not been given to the differing needs of these communities, although where research does exist, this has been addressed in the relevant chapter (see also Fish, 2006, 2007, briefing 12). Other gaps include LGBT carers, domestic abuse in LGBT relationships and housing and homelessness. Readers are referred to Bywaters and Jones (2007) for discussion of HIV/AIDS and to Cosis Brown and Cocker (2011) for discussion about religion and belief.

Making a difference in social work practice was the motivation for introducing work with LGBT people in my teaching and learning in higher education over a decade ago when the social and legislative context was very different. Some students were uncomfortable about the discussions and a number had never met LGBT people who were open about their sexuality. During the first few years, workshop-style sessions were held in a local LGBT centre to encourage students to use the centre as a source of expertise and as a key resource to which they could make referrals (eg one of the groups offered support for young people who were coming out and another group was a resource for LGBT parents). The workshop sessions were interactive and many of the exercises focused on LGBT people's rights and their contested entitlements to public services.

When the teaching was relocated to the university, I took the opportunity to include theory-informed discussions about homophobia and heterosexism, which were often related to contemporary national or international events (eg the struggle to achieve marriage equality, homophobic hate crime, the 'It gets better' campaign). These discussions informed a theoretical examination of heterosexism in a think-piece that was included in a special issue of the journal *Social Work Education* (Fish, 2008a). Issues from practice were highlighted through resources such as the *Opening Doors* report produced by Age Concern (now Age UK) (Smith and Calvert, 2001), the work of the

Albert Kennedy Trust in supporting young homeless LGBT people and the Alzheimer's Society's work with LGBT carers, and this was subsequently published in *Practice: Social Work in Action* (Fish, 2009a). Increasing attention to evidence-based practice in social work to underpin assessments and decisions about interventions has meant that the need for peer-reviewed research has become more pressing. But a recent report by the Equality and Human Rights Commission – *How Fair is Britain?* (EHRC, 2010) – found that there was a lack of peer-reviewed research across a number of domains including social care, health and education. One of the primary aims in writing this book has been to bring together current research with LGBT people and to critically reflect on its implications for social work. Social work as a profession has a long-standing commitment to challenging oppression, but sometimes students lack confidence or knowledge about the most appropriate course of action.

Current context

The introduction of the Equality Act 2010 and the subsequent implementation of the public-sector equality duty means that there is now a legislative requirement for public bodies to assess the impact of their decisions on people of different backgrounds (including LGBT people) and to promote equality and good relations between them (EHRC, 2010). In June 2010, the newly elected Coalition government outlined its planned commitment to LGBT equalities in a Government Equalities Office policy document (HMG, 2010a). The document identified a programme of work to tackle outdated prejudices and ensure equal chances for everyone whatever their sexual orientation and gender identity, including in schools, workplaces, family life and public services, participation in civil society, tackling homophobic hate crime, and asylum. It included a commitment to address global inequalities for LGBT people in support of the United Nations statement that sexual orientation and gender identity should not form the basis for criminal penalties.

History suggests that legislation alone will not achieve equal outcomes in people's everyday lives; for example, despite the introduction of the Equal Pay Act in 1970, the pay gap between men and women is 'stubbornly persistent' (EHRC, 2010: 410). Although it is no longer socially acceptable to express prejudice, a national survey found that almost a quarter of respondents said they 'sometimes feel prejudice [towards LGBT people] but try not to let it show' (Abrams, in EHRC, 2010: 36). Social workers cannot compartmentalise their values and provide an equitable service for LGBT people. But it is not only prejudicial attitudes that impact on the services LGBT people receive; values are reflected in positive action to implement equality in service delivery. The lack of action indicates a low priority afforded to sexual orientation and gender identity and this was evidenced in a government inspection report of older people's residential care homes which found that 'only 7% of providers had worked specifically on equality for LGBT people' (EHRC, 2010: 538).

Voluntary- and community-sector organisations (VCSOs) have often been at the forefront of changing public perceptions and influencing policy development, and they have undertaken a key role in providing appropriate services that have often not been available through the statutory sector. A recent lottery-funded project found that although the sector in London received only 0.06% of total VCSO income, it was engaged in a diverse range of projects offering advocacy, community building and skills development (Kairos in Soho, 2011). Current changes in the delivery of welfare and cuts to funding may have a disproportionate impact on the sector, which has been built up over the last three decades. The current context holds the promise of a secure legislative basis for LGBT equality but also the potential threat to existing services and expertise.

It is intended that this book makes a compelling case for social work students and practitioners to further develop their values, skills and knowledge in their practice with LGBT individuals, families and communities and to see this as an ongoing journey.

Glossary

Anti-discriminatory practice is a fundamental approach in social work that aims to empower service users to challenge inequalities in their everyday lives and work with them to address them.

Asylum is the protection given by a country to someone who is fleeing persecution in their own country. Asylum is granted under the 1951 UN Convention Relating to the Status of Refugees.

Asylum process: there are six stages to the process of making a legal claim for asylum in the UK: the asylum screening interview, being allocated a case owner, the personal interview, the period when the decision is made (which can take six months) and the decision. Successful applicants are granted refugee status and are given discretionary leave to remain, which is temporary permission to stay in the UK, usually for a period of three years. At the end of this period, the case is reviewed to assess whether the social and political environment in the country of origin continues to represent a risk of persecution. Unsuccessful applicants are expected to return to their country of origin and this may be a voluntary or forcible return.

Asylum seeker is someone who has asked for protection but is awaiting a decision to be recognised as a refugee or waiting for the outcome of an appeal.

Asylum support: the UK Border Agency provides support to asylum seekers in the form of accommodation and subsistence. If they have additional care needs, due to chronic illness or disability, asylum seekers may also be eligible for support from their local authority.

Case owner: this is the person from the UKBA to whom the applicant is allocated. The case owner deals with every aspect of the claim and is the single point of contact for the claimant and their legal representative.

Coming out refers to the process of acknowledging and identifying oneself as lesbian, gay or bisexual and disclosing this to others. Coming out as non-heterosexual is necessary because of widespread assumptions of heterosexuality. It has often been considered to be a political act.

Discretionary leave to remain: this is temporary permission to remain in the UK, usually for a period of three years.

Dispersal: the Immigration and Asylum Act 1999 introduced measures which mean that asylum seekers are accommodated outside of London and the South East.

Equality: equal treatment does not mean that everyone is treated in the same way, but rather that everyone is offered the same standard of treatment, which may differ according to their particular concerns and needs.

Exceptional leave to remain: if an application for asylum has been refused, the applicant may be granted permission to stay on humanitarian grounds.

Gender Identity Disorder (GID) (also known as gender dysphoria): this is the diagnostic category in the Diagnostic and Statistical Manual used to assess whether someone can access gender reassignment surgery. A GID diagnosis means that someone has a strong and persistent cross–gender identification and discomfort about the sex they were assigned at birth. Many trans people feel that in order to access surgery, they must be diagnosed with a mental health problem and are seeking to change the criteria.

Heterocentric is a concept developed in queer theory that constructs heterosexuality as natural and normal and refers to the social privilege afforded to heterosexuality.

Heteronormativity is a similar concept to heterocentric and refers to a social and cultural worldview that constructs heterosexuality as the norm.

Heterosexism is a system of beliefs which assume that everyone is heterosexual. It assumes the superiority of heterosexuality; for example, it assumes that families comprising an opposite-sex couple are inherently superior to same-sex family relationships.

Homophobia has been commonly used to describe the oppression and discrimination experienced by LGBT people. It has often been used to refer to extreme acts of anti–gay violence such as hate crimes.

Indefinite leave to remain: permanent residence may be given after the initial qualifying period if asylum seekers are granted continuing status.

Intersectionality is used to acknowledge that people occupy a range of social positions or multiple identities: for example, someone may be a gay man and working class, they may be a trans person and a father. An intersectional approach recognises that people's experiences of discrimination and privilege are affected by the different social positions they occupy.

Lesbian, gay, bisexual and trans people (LGBT): the acronym LGBT entered into common usage in the late 1990s to identify a social and political alliance campaigning for social and legal change. Although there are many differences between them, the term represents an inclusive approach to social change.

Men who have sex with men refers to men who have sexual relationships with other men but do not identify as gay or bisexual.

No recourse to public funds (NRPF) refers to people who are subject to immigration control and have no entitlement to welfare benefits, UK Border Agency support or public housing. However, social services departments may have a duty to provide services (including accommodation) to people with NRPF who meet thresholds for support under community care or human rights legislation. An asylum seeker whose claim has failed is not eligible for support if they have failed to comply with removal directions.

Queer theory is a body of critical theory that critiques the binary heterosexual–homosexual model of sexuality and heteronormative assumptions about, for example, the nature of relationships or family formations. It was influenced by the work of the French theorist Michel Foucault (1978). Notable queer theorists include Judith Butler, Eve Kosovsky-Sedgwick, Diana Fuss and Jeffrey Weeks.

Refugee Integration and Employment Service (RIES): this is a 12-month service to each person granted refugee status or humanitarian protection. It includes: an advice and support service for housing, education and access to benefits; employment advice; and a mentoring service.

Refugee status: a refugee is an individual to whom the UK government has offered protection in accordance with the 1951 Refugee Convention and granted leave to stay.

Sexual orientation is the term used to describe someone's identity, attraction, behaviour or community affiliations. 'Heterosexual', 'lesbian', 'gay' and 'bisexual' are all terms used to describe someone's sexual orientation, sexual identity and sexual preference.

Trans people: in the UK, the term trans is used to describe everyone with gender non-conforming behaviour or presentation. In North America, the term transgender is preferred.

Transphobia refers to the specific discrimination and oppression experienced by trans people. Although protection from discrimination in employment and access to public services has been legislated for, many trans people continue to experience prejudicial attitudes and behaviour towards their gender identity. This can have an impact on their employment, housing, personal relationships and safety.

Transitioning refers to the process of changing gender presentation from the sex assigned at birth to the acquired gender. Transitioning refers to any part or the whole process of changing gender: some people may choose not to have surgery.

United Kingdom Border Agency (UKBA): this is the section of the Home Office that considers applications for permission to enter or stay in the UK as an asylum seeker. The UKBA is responsible for the accommodation and support of asylum seekers.

References

Abbott, D. and Howarth, J. (2005) *Secret Loves, Hidden Lives: Exploring Issues for People with Learning Difficulties who are Gay, Lesbian or Bisexual*. Bristol: The Policy Press.

Adams, C.L.J. and Kimmel, D.C. (1997) 'Exploring the lives of older African American gay men', in B. Greene (ed) *Ethnic and Cultural Diversity among Lesbians and Gay Men* (pp 132–51), Thousand Oaks, CA: Sage Publications.

Alleyn, C. and Jones, R.L. (2010) 'Queerying care: Dissident trans identities in health and social care', in R.L. Jones and R. Ward (eds) *LGBT Issues: Looking Beyond Categories: Policy and Practice in Health and Social Care* (pp 42–55), Edinburgh: Dunedin Academic Press.

Almack, K., Seymour, J. and Bellamy, G. (2010) 'Exploring the impact of sexual orientation on experiences and concerns about end of life care and on bereavement for lesbian, gay and bisexual elders', *Sociology*, 44, 908–24.

Amnesty International (2001) *Crimes of Hate, Conspiracy of Silence: Torture and Ill-Treatment Based on Sexual Identity*, London: Amnesty International.

Austin, S.B., Ziyadeh, N., Kahn, J.A., Camargo, C.A., Colditz, G.A. and Field, A.E. (2004) 'Sexual orientation, weight concerns, and eating-disordered behaviors in adolescent girls and boys', *Journal of the American Academy of Child and Adolescent Psychiatry*, 43, 1115–23.

Baiocco, R., D'Alessio, M. and Laghi, F. (2010) 'Binge drinking among gay, and lesbian youths: the role of internalized sexual stigma, self-disclosure, and individuals' sense of connectedness to the gay community', *Addictive Behaviors*, 35, 896–9.

BASW (British Association of Social Workers) (2002) *Code of Ethics for Social Workers*, Birmingham: BASW.

Bayliss, K. (2000) 'Social work values, anti-discriminatory practice and working with older lesbian service users', *Social Work Education*, 19, 45–53.

Beddoes, D., Sheikh, S., Pralat, R. and Sloman, J. (2010) *The Impact of Drugs on Different Minority Groups: A Review of the UK Literature. Part 2: Lesbian, Gay, Bisexual and Transgender (LGBT) Groups*, London: The UK Drug Policy Commission (UKDPC).

Bell, M. and Hansen, C. (2009) *Over Not Out: The Housing and Homelessness Issues Specific to Lesbian, Gay, Bisexual and Transgender Asylum Seekers*, London: Refugee Support.

Ben-Ari, A.T. (2001) 'Homosexuality and heterosexism: views from academics in the helping professions', *British Journal of Social Work*, 31, 119–31.

Beresford, P. (no date) *Access to Social Care: Shaping Our Lives. Human Rights: Transforming Services,* London: SCIE. Available at: www.scie.org.uk (accessed 8 September 2010).

Beyond Barriers (2002) *First Out: Report of the Beyond Barriers Survey of Lesbian, Gay, Bisexual and Transgender People in Scotland,* Edinburgh: Beyond Barriers.

Bhugra, D. (1997) 'Coming out by South Asian gay men in the United Kingdom', *Archives of Sexual Behavior*, 25, 547–57.

BIHR (British Institute of Human Rights) (2007a) *Human Rights in Health Care: A Framework for Local Action,* London: Department of Health.

BIHR (2007b) 'Human Rights Act: changing lives'. Available at: http://www.bihr.org.uk/sites/default/files/BIHR%20Changing%20Lives%20FINAL_0.pdf

Boehmer, U. (2002) 'Twenty years of public health research: inclusion of lesbian, gay, bisexual, and transgender populations', *American Journal of Public Health*, 92, 1125–30.

Bowcott, O. (2011) 'Couple win landmark case against hotel that refused double bed', *The Guardian*, 19 January, pp 11–12.

Brothers, M. (2003) 'Not just ramps and Braille: disability and sexual orientation', in K. E. Zappone (ed) *Re-thinking Identity: The Challenge of Diversity*, Dublin: Joint Equality and Human Rights Forum, pp 49–64. Available at: http://www.ihrc.ie (accessed 26 February 2007).

Browne, K. and Lim, J. (2008a) *Count Me In Too: Mental Health.* Brighton: Spectrum.

Browne, K. and Lim, J. (2008b) *Trans People: Additional Findings Report. Count Me in Too: LGBT Lives in Brighton and Hove*, Brighton: Spectrum.

Browne, K., McGlynn, N. and Lim, J. (2009) *Drugs and Alcohol – Additional Findings Report: Count Me In Too: LGBT Lives in Brighton and Hove*, Brighton: Spectrum.

Buffin, J. and Mirza, I. (2009) *Outing Notts: A Study into the Substance Misuse Needs and Experiences of LGBT People across Nottinghamshire*, Preston: University of Central Lancashire with Safer Nottingham Drug and Alcohol Team.

Burns, C. (2008) 'Trans: a practical guide for the NHS'. Available at: http://www.dh.gov.uk/prod_consum_dh/groups/dh_digitalassets/@dh/@en/documents/digitalasset/dh_089939.pdf (accessed 12 April 2010).

Buttoo, S. (2010) 'Gay Asians reveal racism problems'. Available at: http://news.bbc.co.uk/1/hi/uk/8555503.stm (accessed 11 January 2011).

Bywaters, J. and Jones, R. (2007) *Sexuality and Social Work,* Exeter: Learning Matters.

Calma, T. (2008) 'The role of social workers as human rights workers with Indigenous people and communities', Australian Human Rights Commission. Available at: http://www.hreoc.gov.au/about/media/speeches/social_justice/2008/20080212_socialwork.html (accessed 8 September 2010).

Cass, V.C. (1979) 'Homosexual identity formation: a theoretical model', *Journal of Homosexuality*, 4, 219–35.

Castagnoli, C. (2010) *Transgender Persons' Rights in the EU Member States.* Brussels: European Parliament, Citizens' Rights and Constitutional Affairs.

CCETSW (Central Council for Education and Training in Social Work) (1991) *DipSW: Rules and Requirements for the Diploma in Social Work. Paper 30*, London: CCETSW.

Cemlyn, S. (2008) 'Human rights and Gypsies and Travellers: an exploration of the application of a human rights perspective to social work with a minority community in Britain', *British Journal of Social Work*, 38, 153–73.

Centre for Human Rights (1994) *Human Rights and Social Work: A Manual for Schools of Social Work and the Social Work Profession*, New York and Geneva: United Nations.

Chan, C.S. (1997) 'Don't ask, don't tell, don't know: the formation of a homosexual identity and sexual expression among Asian American lesbians', in B. Greene (ed) *Ethnic and Cultural Diversity among Lesbians and Gay Men*, pp 229–52, Thousand Oaks, CA: Sage Publications.

Charnley, H.M. and Langley, J. (2007) 'Developing cultural competence as a framework for anti-heterosexist practice: reflections from the UK', *Journal of Social Work*, 7, 307–21.

ChildLine (2001) *Saving Young Lives: Calls to ChildLine about Suicide*, London: ChildLine.

Clements, L. (no date) *Access to Justice: Human Rights Poverty and Social Exclusion. Human Rights: Transforming Services,* London: SCIE. Available at: www.scie.org.uk (accessed 8 September 2010).

CLG (Department for Communities and Local Government) and DCSF (Department for Children, Schools and Families) (2010) *Provision of Accommodation for 16 and 17 Year Old Young People who may be Homeless and/or Require Accommodation*, London: DSCF.

Cochran, B.N. and Cauce, A.M. (2006) 'Characteristics of lesbian, gay, bisexual, and transgender individuals entering substance abuse treatment', *Journal of Substance Abuse Treatment*, 30, 135–46.

Cochran, S.D. and Mays, V.M. (1988) 'Disclosure of sexual preference to physicians by black lesbian and bisexual women', *Western Journal of Medicine*, 149, 616–19.

Cochran, S.D. and Mays, V.M. (2000) 'Relation between Psychiatric Syndromes and Behaviorally Defined Sexual Orientation in a Sample of the US Population', *American Journal of Epidemiology*, 151(5), 516–23.

Cochran, S.D., Mays, V.M. and Sullivan, J.G. (2003) 'Prevalence of mental disorders, psychological distress, and mental health services use among lesbian, gay, and bisexual adults in the United States', *Journal of Consulting and Clinical Psychology*, 71(1): 53-61.

Concannon, L. (2009) 'Developing inclusive health and social care policies for older LGBT citizens', *The British Journal of Social Work*, 39, 403–17.

Congress, E. (2006) 'Teaching social work values, ethics and human rights'. Available at: http://www.ifsw.org (accessed 16 June 2010).

Consolacion, T.B., Russell, S.T. and Sue, S. (2004) 'Sex, race/ethnicity, and romantic attractions: multiple minority status adolescents and mental health', *Cultural Diversity and Ethnic Minority Psychology*, 10, 200–14.

Cosis Brown, H. and Cocker, C. (2011) *Social Work with Lesbians and Gay Men*, London: Sage Publications.

CPS (Crown Prosecution Service) (2009) *Policy for Prosecuting Cases of Homophobic and Transphobic Crime,* London: CPS.

Cree, V. and Myers, S. (2008) *Social Work: Making a Difference*, Bristol: The Policy Press.

Cross, W.E. (1991) *Shades of Black: Diversity in African-American Identity*, Philadelphia: Temple University Press.

Croucher, K. (2008) *Housing Choices and Aspirations of Older People: Research from the New Horizons Programme*, London: Department for Communities and Local Government.

CSCI (Commission for Social Care Inspection) (2008) *Putting People First: Providing Appropriate Services for Lesbian, Gay and Bisexual and Transgender People*, London: Commission for Social Care Inspection.

Cull, M., Platzer, H. and Balloch, S. (2006) *Out On My Own: Understanding the Experiences and Needs of Homeless Lesbian, Gay, Bisexual and Transgender Youth*, Brighton: Health and Social Policy Research Centre, University of Brighton.

Cutts, R. and Park, C.W. (2009) 'Religious involvement among black men self-labeling as gay', *Journal of Gay and Lesbian Social Services*, 21, 232–46.

Dalrymple, J. and Burke, B. (1995) *Anti-Oppressive Practice: Social Care and the Law*, Buckingham: Open University Press.

Davis, C. (2008) 'Social work practice with transgender and gender nonconforming people', in G.P. Mallon (ed) *Social Work Practice with Lesbian, Gay, Bisexual and Transgender People*, pp 83–111, New York: Routledge.

DCA (Department for Constitutional Affairs) (2006) *Human Rights: A Handbook for Public Authorities*, London: Department for Constitutional Affairs.

de Gruchy, J. and Fish, J. (2004) 'Doctors' involvement in human rights abuses of men who have sex with men in Egypt', *The Lancet*, 363, 1903.

de Jong, J. (2003) *Lesbian, Gay, Bisexual and Transgender (LGBT) Refugees and Asylum Seekers*, London: Information Centre about Asylum and Refugees in the UK (ICAR).

DfES (Department for Education and Skills) and DH (Department of Health) (2008) *The Mental Health and Psychological Wellbeing of Children and Young People*, London: Department of Health.

DH (Department of Health) (1998) *Modernising Mental Health Services*, London: Department of Health.

DH (1999) *The National Service Framework for Mental Health*, London: Department of Health.

DH (2000a) *Framework for the Assessment of Children in Need and Their Families*. London: Stationery Office.

DH (2000b) *Assessing Children and Their Families: Practice Guidance*, London: Stationery Office.

DH (2001a) *Guidance for Field Social Workers, Residential Social Workers and Foster Carers on Providing Information and Referring Young People to Contraceptive and Sexual Health Services*, London: Teenage Pregnancy Unit.

DH (2001b) *Valuing People: A New Strategy for Learning Disability for the 21st Century*, London: Department of Health.

DH (2003) *Care Homes for Older People: National Minimum Standards*, London: Department of Health.

DH (2007) *Putting People First: A Shared Vision and Commitment to the Transformation of Adult Social Care*, London: Department of Health.

DH (2008a) *Human Rights in Healthcare: A Short Introduction*, London: Department of Health.

DH (2008b) *End of Life Care Strategy: Promoting High Quality Care for All Adults at the End of Life.* London: Department of Health.

DH (2008c) *Trans: A Practical Guide for the NHS*. Available at http://www.dh.gov.uk/prod_consum_dh/groups/dh_digitalassets/@dh/@en/documents/digitalasset/dh_089939.pdf (accessed 13 December 2011).

DH (2008d) *The Code of Practice for the Mental Health Act 1983*. Available at http://www.dh.gov.uk/prod_consum_dh/groups/dh_digitalassets/@dh/@en/documents/digitalasset/dh_087073.pdf (accessed 14 December 2011).

DH (2009) *New Horizons: A Shared Vision for Mental Health*, London: Department of Health.

DH (2010a) *National Cancer Patient Experience Survey*, London: Department of Health.

DH (2010b) *Equity and Excellence: Liberating the NHS 2010*, London: Department of Health.

DH (2010c) *A Vision for Adult Social Care: Capable Communities and Active Citizens*, London: DH.

Diaz, R.M., Ayala, G., Bein, D.E., Henne, J. and Marin, B.V. (2001) 'The impact of homophobia, poverty, and racism on the mental health of gay and bisexual Latino men: findings from 3 US cities', *American Journal of Public Health*, 91, 927–32.

di Ceglie, D. (2010) 'Gender identity and sexuality: what's in a name?', *Diversity in Health Care*, 7, 83–6.

Dick, S. (2008) *Homophobic Hate Crime: The Gay British Crime Survey*, London: Stonewall.

Dominelli, L. (1988) *Anti-Racist Social Work,* Basingstoke: MacMillan Press.

Dunne, G.A. (1997) *Lesbian Lifestyles: Women's Work and the Politics of Sexuality*, Basingstoke: Macmillan.

EHRC (Equality and Human Rights Commission) (2007a) 'Provision of good facilities and services to trans people. Guidance for public authorities'. Available at: http://www.equalityhumanrights.com/uploaded_files/PSD/psd_trans_guidance.pdf (accessed 12 April 2010).

EHRC (2007b) *Provision of Goods, Facilities and Services to Trans People. Guidance for Public Authorities: Meeting Your Equality Duties and Human Rights Obligations*, Manchester: EHRC.

EHRC (2008) 'Ours to own: understanding human rights'. Available at: http://www.equalityhumanrights.com/uploaded_files/ours_to_own_final.pdf (accessed 14 September 2010).

EHRC (2009) 'Beyond tolerance: making sexual orientation a public matter'. Available at: http://www.equalityhumanrights.com/uploaded_files/research/beyond_tolerance.pdf (accessed 8 September 2010).

EHRC (2010) *How Fair is Britain? Equality, Human Rights and Good Relations in 2010,* Manchester: EHRC.

Eisenberg, M.E. and Resnick, M.D. (2006) 'Suicidality among gay, lesbian and bisexual youth: the role of protective factors', *Journal of Adolescent Health*, 39(5), 662–8.

Eisenberg, M.E. and Wechsler, H. (2003) 'Social influences on substance-use behaviors of gay, lesbian, and bisexual college students: findings from a national study', *Social Science and Medicine*, 57, 1913–23.

Ekins, R. and King, D. (1997) 'Blending genders: contributions to the emerging field of transgender studies', *The International Journal of Transgenderism*, 1, 1–10.

ELENA (European Council on Refugees and Exiles) (1997) 'Research paper on sexual orientation as a ground for refugee status'. Available at: http://www.unhcr.org/refworld/docid/3decd1fa4.html (accessed 12 December 2010).

Ellis, B. (1995) *The Experiences of Disabled Women*, York: Joseph Rowntree Foundation.

Ellison, G. and Gunstone, B. (2009) *Sexual Orientation Explored: a Study of Identity, Attraction, Behaviour and Attitudes in 2009*. Manchester: YouGov and Equality and Human Rights Commission.

Fannin, A., Fenge, L., Hicks, C., Lavin, N. and Brown, K. (2008) *Social Work Practice with Older Lesbians and Gay Men*, Exeter: Learning Matters.

Fashanu, J. (1994) 'Strong enough to survive', in E. Healey and A. Mason (eds) *Stonewall 25: The Making of the Lesbian and Gay Community in Britain*, pp 20–5, London: Virago.

Feldman, J. and Bockting, W. (2001) 'Primary care of the transgender patient', paper presented to XVII Harry Benjamin International Gender Dysphoria Association Symposium 31 October–4 November, Galveston, Texas, USA.

Fergusson, D.M., Horwood, L.J. and Beautrais, A.L. (1999) 'Is sexual orientation related to mental health problems and suicidality in young people?', *Archives of General Psychiatry*, 56, 876–80.

Fish, J. (2006) *Heterosexism in Health and Social Care*, Basingstoke: Palgrave.

Fish, J. (2007) 'Getting equal: the implications of new regulations to prohibit sexual orientation discrimination for health and social care', *Diversity in Health and Social Care*, 4(3), 221–8.

Fish, J. (2008a) 'Far from mundane: theorising heterosexism for social work education', *Social Work Education*, 27, 182–93.

Fish, J. (2008b) 'Navigating Queer Street: researching the intersections of lesbian, gay, bisexual and trans (LGBT) identities in health research', *Sociological Research Online*, 13, 1. Available at: http://www.socresonline.org.uk/13/1/12.html

Fish, J. (2009a) 'Invisible no more? Including lesbian, gay bisexual and trans people in social work and social care', *Practice: Social Work in Action*, 21, 48–63.

Fish, J. (2009b) 'All things equal? Social work and lesbian, gay and bisexual global health inequalities', in P. Bywaters, L. Napier and E. McLeod (eds) *Social Work and Global Health Inequalities: Policy and Practice Developments*, pp 144–9, Bristol: The Policy Press.

Fish, J. (2010) '"It's a mixed up, muddled up, shook up world, except for Lola": transforming health and social care for trans people', *Diversity in Health Care*, 7, 87–9.

Fish, J. and Bewley, S. (2010) 'Using human rights based approaches to conceptualise lesbian and bisexual women's health inequalities', *Health and Social Care in the Community*, 18, 355–62.

Fokkema, T. and Kuyper, L. (2009) 'The relation between social embeddedness and loneliness among older lesbian, gay, and bisexual adults in the Netherlands', *Archives of Sexual Behavior*, 38, 264–75.

Forrester, D. and Harwin, J. (2006) 'Parental substance misuse and child care social work: findings from the first stage of a study of 100 families', *Child and Family Social Work*, 11, 325–35.

Foucault, M. (1978) *The History of Sexuality: The Will to Knowledge*, Harmondsworth: Penguin.

FRA (European Union Fundamental Rights Agency) (2009) 'Homophobia and Discrimination on Grounds of Sexual Orientation and Gender Identity in the EU Member States'. Available at: http://www.fra.europa.eu/fraWebsite/attachments/FRA_hdgso_report_Part%202_en.pdf (accessed 27 February 2011).

Furness, S. and Gilligan, P. (2010) *Religion, Belief and Social Work: Making a Difference*, Bristol: The Policy Press.

Galop (2001) *The Low Down: Black Lesbians, Gay Men and Bisexual People talk about their Experiences and Needs*, London: Galop.

Gay and Grey in Dorset (2006) *Lifting the Lid on Sexuality and Ageing*. Bournemouth: Help and Care.

Gerstel, C.J., Feraios, A.J. and Herdt, G. (1989) 'Widening circles: an ethnographic profile of a youth group', in G. Herdt (ed) *Gay and Lesbian Youth*, pp 75–92, New York: The Haworth Press.

Gillespie-Sells, K., Hill, M. and Robbins, B. (eds) (1998) *She Dances to Different Drums: Research into Disabled Women's Sexuality*, London: King's Fund.

Glasgow Anti-Stigma Partnership (2009) *'There's More to Me': A Report on Lesbian, Gay and Bisexual People's Beliefs, Attitudes and Experiences in Mental Health,* Glasgow: Scottish Association for Mental Health.

Glendinning, C., Challis, D., Fernández, J., Jacobs, S., Jones, K., Knapp, M., Netten, A., Stevens, M. and Wilberforce, M. (2008) *Evaluation of the Individual Budgets Pilot Programme*, University of York: Social Policy Research Unit.

Gold, D. (2005) *Sexual Exclusion: Issues and Best Practice in Lesbian, Gay and Bisexual Housing and Homelessness*, London: Stonewall Housing.

Gomez, J.L. and Smith, B. (1994) 'Taking the home out of homophobia: black lesbian health', in M. Wilson (ed) *Healthy and Wise: The Essential Health Handbook for Black Women*, pp 185–204, London: Virago Press.

Goodman, A. (2009) *Social Work with Drug and Substance Misusers*, Exeter: Learning Matters.

Graham, L.F., Braithwaite, K., Spikes, P., Stephens, C.F. and Edu, U.F. (2009) 'Exploring the mental health of black men who have sex with men', *Community Mental Health Journal*, 45, 272–84.

Grant, J.M., Mottet, L.A. and Tanis, J. (2010) *National Transgender Discrimination Survey Report on Health and Health Care*. Washington DC: National Center for Transgender Equality and the National Gay and Lesbian Task Force.

Greene, B. (1997) 'Ethnic minority lesbians and gay men: mental health and treatment issues', in B. Greene (ed) *Ethnic and Cultural Diversity among Lesbians and Gay Men*, pp 216–39, Thousand Oaks, CA: Sage Publications.

Greene, B. (2003) 'Beyond heterosexism and across the cultural divides – developing an inclusive lesbian, gay and bisexual psychology: a look to the future', in L. Garnets and D.C. Kimmel (eds) *Psychological Perspectives on Lesbian, Gay, and Bisexual Experiences*, pp 357–97, New York, NY: Columbia University Press.

GRP (Gender Recognition Panel) (2010) 'Minutes of Gender Recognition Panel, March 2010'. Available at: http://www.grp.gov.uk/documents/grp_minutes_18Mar10.pdf.pdf (accessed 23 September 2010).

Gruskin, E.P., Hart, S., Gordon, N. and Ackerson, L. (2001) 'Patterns of cigarette smoking and alcohol use among lesbians and bisexual women enrolled in a large health maintenance organization', *American Journal of Public Health*, 91, 976–9.

GSCC (General Social Care Council) (2010) *Codes of Practice for Social Care Workers*, London: GSCC.

Gulland, A. (2009) 'Direct payments letting down gay service users', *Community Care*, 11 February, pp 24–5.

Halkitis, P.N. and Jerome, R.C. (2008) 'A comparative analysis of methamphetamine use: black gay and bisexual men in relation to men of other races', *Addictive Behaviors*, 33, 83–93.

Halkitis, P.N., Palamar, J.J. and Mukherjee, P.P. (2007) 'Poly-club-drug use among gay and bisexual men: a longitudinal analysis', *Drug and Alcohol Dependence*, 89, 153–160.

Hardman, K.L.J. (1997) 'Social workers' attitudes to lesbian clients', *British Journal of Social Work*, 27, 545–63.

Hartley, C.F. and Whittle, S. (2003) 'Different sexed and gendered bodies demand different ways of thinking about policy and practice', *Practice: Social Work in Action*, 15, 61–73.

Heaphy, B. (2009) 'The storied, complex lives of older GLBT adults: choice and its limits in older lesbian and gay narratives of relational life', *Journal of GLBT Family Studies*, 5, 119–38.

Heaphy, B., Yip, A. and Thompson, D. (2003) *Lesbian, Gay and Bisexual Lives over 50: A report on the project 'The Social and Policy Implications of Non-heterosexual Ageing'*, Nottingham Trent University: York House Publications.

Heller, P. (2009) 'Challenges facing LGBT asylum-seekers: the role of social work in correcting oppressive immigration processes', *Journal of Gay and Lesbian Social Services*, 21, 294–308.

Herek, G.M. (2000) 'The psychology of sexual prejudice', *Current Directions in Psychological Science*, 9, 19–22.

Hicks, S. (2005) 'Queer genealogies: tales of conformity and rebellion amongst lesbian and gay foster carers and adopters', *Qualitative Social Work: Research and Practice*, 4, 293–308.

Hicks, S. (2008) 'What does social work desire?', *Social Work Education*, 27, 131–7.

Hickson, F., Weatherburn, P., Reid, D., Jessup, K. and Hammond, G. (2009) *Testing Targets: Findings from the United Kingdom Gay Men's Sex Survey*, London: Sigma Research.

Hill, A. (2011) 'Charity challenges disapproval of same-sex parents in survey', *The Guardian*, 31 January, p 12.

Hill, L., Gray, R., Stroud, J. and Chiripanyanga, S. (2009) 'Inter-professional learning to prepare medical and social work students for practice with refugees and asylum seekers', *Social Work Education: the International Journal*, 28, 298–308.

Hinchliffe, S., Gott, M. and Galena, E. (2005) '"I daresay I might find it embarrassing": general practitioners' perspectives on discussing sexual health issues with lesbian and gay patients', *Health and Social Care in the Community*, 13, 345–53.

Hines, S. (2007) 'Transgendering care: practices of care within transgender communities', *Critical Social Policy*, 7, 462–86.

HMG (HM Government) (2009) *Valuing People Now: A New Three-Year Strategy for People with Learning Disabilities*, London: Department of Health.

HMG (2010a) *Working for Lesbian, Gay, Bisexual and Transgender Equality*, London: Government Equalities Office.

HMG (2010b) *Drug Strategy 2010: Reducing Demand, Restricting Supply, Building Recovery.* London: Home Office.

HMG (2010c) *The Coalition: Our Programme for Government.* London: Cabinet Office.

Hoare, J. (2010) 'Annex 2: nationally representative estimates of illicit drug use by self-reported sexual orientation, 2006/07–2008/09 BCS', in Hoare, J. and Moon, D. (eds) *Drug Misuse Declared: Findings from the 2009/10 British Crime Survey*, Home Office Statistical Bulletin 13/10, London: Home Office. Available at: http://www.homeoffice.gov.uk/rds/pdfs10/hosb1310.pdf

Holman, C.W. and Goldberg, J.M. (2006) *Social and Medical Advocacy with Transgender People and Loved Ones: Recommendations for BC Clinicians.* Vancouver, BC: Transcend Transgender Support and Education Society and Vancouver Coastal Health's Transgender Health Program.

Home Office (2008) *Drugs: Protecting Families and Communities 2008-2011*, London: Home Office.

House of Commons Select Committee, Education and Skills (2007) 'Report on bullying'. Available at: http://www.publications.parliament.uk/pa/cm200607/cmselect/cmeduski/85/8502.htm (accessed 2 February 2009).

House of Lords (2008) *The Slough Judgment.* Available at: http://www.publications.parliament.uk/pa/ld200708/ldjudgmt/jd080730/rmfc-1.htm (accessed 14 December).

Hubbard, R. and Rossington, J. (2001) *As We Grow Older: A Study of the Housing and Support Needs of Older Lesbians and Gay Men*, Polari Housing Association.

Hughes, T.L. and Jacobson, K.M. (2003) 'Sexual orientation and women's smoking', *Current Women's Health Report*, 3, 254–61.

Hughes, T.L., Johnson, T. and Wilsnack, S.C. (2001) 'Sexual assault and alcohol abuse: a comparison of lesbians and heterosexual women', *Journal of Substance Abuse*, 13, 515–32.

Hull, G.T., Scott, P.B. and Smith, B. (eds) (1982) *All the Women Are White, All the Blacks Are Men, but Some of Us Are Brave: Black Women's Studies*, Old Westbury, NY: Feminist Press.

Hunt, R. and Jensen, J. (2007) *The School Report: The Experiences of Young Gay People in Britain's Schools*. London: Stonewall.

Hunt, R. and Fish, J. (2008) *Prescription for Change: Lesbian and Bisexual Women's Health and Social Care Survey*, London: Stonewall.

Ife, J. (2001) 'Local and global practice: relocating social work as a human rights profession in the new global order', *European Journal of Social Work*, 4, 5–15.

IFSW (International Federation of Social Workers) and IASSW (International Association of Schools of Social Work) (2004) *Ethics in Social Work: Statement of Principles*, Berne, Switzerland: IFSW.

IGLHRC (International Gay and Lesbian Human Rights Commission) (2010) *The Violation of the Rights of Lesbian, Gay, Bisexual and Transgender Persons in El Salvador*, New York: Shadow Report to the United Nations Human Rights Committee.

International Service for Human Rights (2007) 'Yogyakarta principles on the application of international human rights law in relation to sexual orientation and gender identity'. Available at: http://www.yogyakartaprinciples.org/principles_en.pdf (accessed 4 March 2009).

Jefferson, G. and Tkaczuk, N. (2005) *Outing Drugs: Report of the Community-Led Research Project Focusing on Drug and Alcohol Use by Gay Men's Health Wiltshire and Swindon amongst the Gay and Bisexual Male Communities in Wiltshire and Swindon*, Swindon: Gay Men's Health.

Johnson, K., Faulkner, P., Jones, H. and Welsh, E. (2007) *Understanding Suicide and Promoting Survival in LGBT Communities*, Brighton: University of Brighton.

Johnson, S. (2005) *Residential and Community Care of Transgender People*. London: The Beaumont Society.

Kahn, P. and O'Rourke, K. (2005) *Guide to Curriculum Design: Enquiry-Based Learning*. Manchester: University of Manchester.

Kairos in Soho (2011) 'The London LGBT voluntary and community sector almanac'. Available at: http://www.kairosinsoho.org.uk/KISalmanacRGB.pdf (accessed 11 August 2011).

Kaminski, P.L., Chapman, B.J., Haynes, S.D. and Own, L. (2005) 'Body image, eating behaviors, and attitudes toward exercise among gay and straight men', *Eating Behaviors*, 6, 179–87.

Kelly, A. (2009) 'Raped and killed for being a lesbian: South Africa ignores "corrective" attacks', *The Guardian*, 12 March. Available at: http://www.guardian.co.uk/world/2009/mar/12/eudy-simelane-corrective-rape-south-africa

Kenagy, G.P. (2005) 'Transgender health: findings from two needs assessment studies in Philadelphia', *Health and Social Work*, 31, 19–26.

Keogh, P., Reid, D. and Weatherburn, P. (2006) *Lambeth LGBT Matters: The Needs and Experiences of Lesbians, Gay Men, Bisexual and Trans Men and Women in Lambeth*, London: Sigma Research.

Keogh, P., Reid, D., Bourne, A., Weatherburn, P., Hickson, F., Jessup, K. and Hammond, G. (2009) *Wasted Opportunities: Problematic Alcohol and Drug Use among Gay Men and Bisexual Men*, London: Sigma Research.

Kessel, A. (2009) 'Gold medal athlete Caster Semenya told to prove she is a woman', *The Guardian*. Available at: http://www.guardian.co.uk/sport/2009/aug/19/caster-semenya-gender-verification-test

Kessler, S. and McKenna, W. (2000) 'Gender construction in everyday life', *Feminism and Psychology*, 10, 11–29.

King, M. (2008) 'Systematic review of mental health and DSH in lesbian, gay and bisexual people', Paper presented to National LGBT Mental health conference, Nottingham, 28 May.

King, M. and Bartlett, A. (2006) 'What same sex civil partnerships may mean for health', *Journal of Epidemiology and Community Health*, 60, 188–91.

King, M. and McKeown, E. (2003) *Mental Health and Social Wellbeing of Gay Men, Lesbians and Bisexuals in England and Wales*, London: MIND.

King, M., McKeown, E., Warner, J., Ramsay, A., Johnson, K. and Cort, C. (2003) 'Mental health and quality of life of gay men and lesbians in England and Wales: controlled, cross-sectional study', *British Journal of Psychiatry*, 183, 552–8.

King, M., Smith, G. and Bartlett, A. (2004) 'Treatments of homosexuality in Britain since the 1950s – an oral history: the experience of professionals', *British Medical Journal*, 328(7437), 429–441.

King, M., Semlyen, J., See Tai, S., Killaspy, H., Osborn, D. and Popelyuk, D. (2007) *Mental Disorders, Suicide, and Deliberate Self Harm in Lesbian, Gay and Bisexual People*. London: National Institute for Mental Health England.

Kinsey, A.C., Pomeroy, W.B., Martin, C.E. and Gebhard, P.H. (1953) *Sexual Behavior in the Human Female*, Philadelphia, PA: W.B. Saunders Company.

Kitzinger, C. (1987) *The Social Construction of Lesbianism*, London: Sage.

Knocker, S. (2006) *The Whole of Me: Meeting the Needs of Older Lesbians, Gay Men and Bisexuals Living in Care Homes and Extra Care Housing*. London: Age Concern.

Kolb, D.A. (1984) *Experiential Learning*, New York: Prentice Hall.

Kosovsky Sedgwick, E. (1993) 'Epistemology of the closet', in H. Abelove, M.A. Barale and D.M. Halperin (eds) *The Lesbian and Gay Studies Reader*, pp 45–61, London: Routledge.

Laird, N. and Aston, L. (2003) *Participatory Appraisal Transgender Research*. Glasgow: Beyond Barriers.

Laumann, E.O., Gagnon, J.H., Michael, R.T. and Michaels, S. (1994) *The Social Organization of Sexuality: Sexual Practices in the United States*. Chicago: University of Chicago Press.

Logan, J., Kershaw, S., Karban, K., Mills, S., Trotter, J. and Sinclair, M. (1996) *Confronting Prejudice: Lesbian and Gay Issues in Social Work Education*, Aldershot: Arena.

Lorde, A. (1984) *Sister Outsider: Essays and Speeches*, Freedom, CA: The Crossing Press.

Luft, J. and Ingham, H. (1955) 'The Johari window, a graphic model of interpersonal awareness', Proceedings of the Western Training Laboratory in group development, Los Angeles: University of California at Los Angeles.

Lukins, M. (2008) 'if every child matters what about us? Young people's experiences of homophobic bullying in Southampton schools', unpublished dissertation, Southampton.

MacFarlane, L. (1998) *Diagnosis Homophobic: The Experiences of Lesbians, Gay Men and Bisexuals in Mental Health Services*, London: PACE.

Mallon, G.P. (ed) (2008) *Social Work Practice with Lesbian, Gay, Bisexual and Transgender People*, New York: Routledge.

Mao, L., McCormick, J. and Van der Ven, P. (2002) 'Ethnic and gay identification: gay Asian men dealing with the divide', *Culture, Health and Sexuality*, 4, 419–30.

Martin, J. (2007) *Safeguarding Adults*, Lyme Regis: Russell House Publishing.

Mason-John, V. (1995) *Talking Black: Lesbians of African and Asian Descent Speak Out*, London: Cassell.

Mays, V.M. and Cochran, S.D. (2001) 'Mental health correlates of perceived discrimination among lesbian, gay, and bisexual adults in the United States', *American Journal of Public Health*, 91, 1869–76.

Mays, V.M., Cochran, S. and Rhue, S. (1993) 'The impact of perceived discrimination on the intimate relationships of black lesbians', *Journal of Homosexuality*, 25, 1–14.

McCabe, S.E., Bostwick, W.B., Hughes, T.L., West, B.T. and Boyd, C.J. (2010) 'The relationship between discrimination and substance use disorders among lesbian, gay, and bisexual adults in the United States', *American Journal of Public Health*, 100, 1946–52.

McDermott, E., Roen, K. and Scourfield, J. (2008) 'Avoiding shame: young LGBT people, homophobia and self-destructive behaviours', *Culture, Health and Sexuality*, 10(8), 815–29.

McFadden, D. and Pasanen, E.G. (1998) 'Comparison of the auditory systems of heterosexuals and homosexuals: click–evoked otoacoustic emissions', *Proceedings of the National Academy of Sciences*, 95, 2709–13.

McKeown, E., Nelson, S., Anderson, J., Low, N. and Elford, J. (2010) 'Disclosure, discrimination and desire: experiences of black and South Asian gay men in Britain', *Culture, Health and Sexuality*, 12, 843–56.

MetLife (2006) *Out and Aging: The MetLife Study of Lesbian and Gay Baby Boomers.* Westport, CT: MetLife Mature Market Institute.

Meyer, I. (2003) 'Prejudice, social stress, and mental health in lesbian, gay, and bisexual populations: conceptual issues and research evidence', *Psychological Bulletin*, 129, 674–97.

Miles, N. (2010) *No Going Back: Lesbian and Gay People and the Asylum System,* London: Stonewall.

Mishna, F., Newman, P.A., Daley, A. and Solomon, S. (2009) 'Bullying of lesbian and gay youth: a qualitative investigation', *British Journal of Social Work*, 39, 1578–1614.

Molloy, D., Knight, T. and Woodfield, K. (2003) *Diversity in Disability: Exploring the Interactions between Disability, Ethnicity, Age, Gender and Sexuality*, Research Report 188, London: Department for Work and Pensions.

Morrison, C. (2008) *Our Journey: Child Protection and LGBT Young People.* Edinburgh: LGBT Youth Scotland.

Mulé, N.J. (2006) 'Equity vs invisibility: sexual orientation issues in social work ethics and curricula standards', *Social Work Education*, 25, 608–22.

Myers, S. (2008) *Solution Focused Approaches*, Lyme Regis: Russell House.

National Disability Authority (2005) *Disability and Sexual Orientation: a Discussion Paper.* Dublin: National Disability Authority.

Nawyn, S.J., Richman, J.A., Rospenda, K.M. and Hughes, T.L. (2000) 'Sexual identity and alcohol-related outcomes: contributions of workplace harassment', *Journal of Substance Abuse*, 11, 289–304.

Newbigging, K., Thomas, N., Coupe, J., Habte-Mariam, Z., Ahmed, N., Shah, A. and Hicks, J. (2010) *Good Practice in Social Care with Refugees and Asylum Seekers.* London: Social Care Institute for Excellence.

Newman, R. (2005) 'Partners in care: being equally different: lesbian and gay carers', *Psychiatric Bulletin*, 29, 266–7.

NMHDU (National Mental Health Development Unit) (2008) *National Suicide Prevention Strategy England: Annual Report of Progress 2008.* Available at: http://www.nmhdu.org.uk/silo/files/national-suicide-prevention-strategy-for-england--annual-report-on-progress-2008.pdf (accessed 24 November 2009).

Noret, N. and Rivers, I. (2003) 'Drug and alcohol use among LGBTs in the City of Leeds', *Social Inclusion & Diversity Research into Practice*, York, St John College.

NTA (National Treatment Agency) (2006) *Models of Care for Treatment of Adult Drug Misusers*, London: Department of Health and Home Office.

Nyman, D. (2000) 'A deaf-gay man', in G. Taylor and J. Bishop (eds) *Being Deaf: The Experiences of Deafness,* pp 173–6, London: Pinter Press and the Open University.

O'Connell, B. (2007) *Solution-focused Therapy*, London: Sage.

OSCE (Organization for Security and Co-operation in Europe) (2009) 'Hate crimes in the OSCE region'. Available at: osce.org (accessed 22 December 2009).

Ottosson, D. (2010) *State-sponsored Homophobia: A World Survey of laws Prohibiting Same Sex Activity Between Consenting Adults*, Brussels, Belgium: International Lesbian and Gay Association. Available at: www.ilga.org (accessed 8 September 2010).

Padilla, Y.C., Crisp, C. and Rew, D.L. (2010) 'Parental acceptance and illegal drug use among gay, lesbian, and bisexual adolescents: results from a national survey', *Social Work*, 55, 265–75.

Parks, C.A., Hughes, T.L. and Matthews, A.K. (2004) 'Race/ethnicity and sexual orientation: intersecting identities', *Cultural Diversity and Ethnic Minority Psychology*, 10, 241–54.

Parrott, B., McIver, A. and Thoburn, J. (2007) *Independent Inquiry Report into the Circumstances of Child Sexual Abuse by Two Foster Carers in Wakefield*, Wakefield: Wakefield Council.

Paul, J.P., Catania, J.P., Pollack, L., Moskowitz, J., Canchola, J., Mills, T. et al (2002) 'Suicide attempts among gay and bisexual men: lifetime prevalence and antecedents', *American Journal of Public Health*, 92, 1338–45.

Peplau, L.A., Cochran, S.D. and Mays, V.M. (1997) 'A national survey of the intimate relationships of African American lesbians and gay men: a look at commitment, satisfaction, sexual behavior, and HIV disease', in B. Greene (ed) *Ethnic and Cultural Diversity among Lesbians and Gay Men*, pp 11–38, Thousand Oaks, CA: Sage Publications.

Phillips, M. and Knocker, S. (2010) *Opening Doors Evaluation: The Story So Far*, London: Age Concern.

Pugh, S. (2005) 'Assessing the cultural needs of older lesbians and gay men: implications for practice', *Practice*, 17, 207–18.

Puri, N. (2008) 'Gay Asians "marrying to conform"'. Available at: http://news.bbc.co.uk/1/hi/uk/7234163.stm

Purnell, L. (2000) 'A description of the Purnell model for cultural competence', *Journal of Transcultural Nursing*, 11, 40–6.

QAA (Quality Assurance Agency) (2008) *Subject Benchmark Statement for Social Work*. Available at www.qaa.ac.uk (accessed 16 November 2010.

Quam, J.K., Whitford, G.S., Dziengel, L.E. and Knochel, K.A. (2010) 'Exploring the nature of same-sex relationships', *Journal of Gerontological Social Work*, 53(8), 702–22.

Quarmby, K. (2008) *Getting Away with Murder: Disabled People's Experiences of Hate Crime,* London: Scope.

Rahman, Q., Cockburn, A. and Govier, E. (2006) 'A comparative analysis of functional cerebral asymmetry in lesbian women, heterosexual women, and heterosexual men', *Archives of Sexual Behaviour*, 37, 566–71.

Rainbow Ripples (2006) 'The Rainbow Ripples Report: lesbian, gay and bisexual disabled people's experiences of service provision in Leeds'. Available at: http://www.rainbowripples.org.uk/the_rainbow_ripples_report.pdf (accessed 16 April 2007).

Ramsey, F., Hill, M. and Kellam, C. (2010) *Black Lesbians Matter: an Examination of the Unique Experiences, Perspectives, and Priorities of the Black Lesbian Community*, Sacramento, CA: Zuna Institute. Available at: http://zunainstitute.org/2010/research/blm/blacklesbiansmatter.pdf (accessed 6 January 2011).

Rankin, S., Cowan, T., Morton, J. and Stoakes, P. (2010) *Public Bodies and the Public Sector Duties relating to Transsexual and Transgender People: Report of Findings and Case Studies*, Manchester: Equality and Human Rights Commission.

RCN (Royal College of Nursing) (2005) *Not Just a Friend,* London: Royal College of Nursing and UNISON.

Reed, B., Rhodes, S., Shofield, P. and Wylie, K. (2009) *Gender Variance in the UK: Prevalence, Incidence, Growth and Geographic Distribution*, London: Gender Identity Research and Education Society.

Remafedi, G., French, S., Story, M., Resnick, M.D. and Blum, R. (1998) 'The relationship between suicide risk and sexual orientation: results of a population-based study', *American Journal of Public Health*, 88, 57–60.

Ridge, D., Hee, A. and Minichiello, V. (1999) 'Asian men on the scene: challenges to gay communities', *Journal of Homosexuality*, 36, 43–68.

Rivers, I. (2001) 'The bullying of sexual minorities at school: its nature and long-term correlates', *Educational and Child Psychology*, 18, 32–46.

Rivers, I. (2004) 'Recollections of bullying at school and their long-term implications for lesbians, gay men, and bisexuals', *Crisis: the Journal of Crisis Intervention and Suicide Prevention*, 25, 169–75.

Roche, A., Morton, J. and Ritchie, G. (2010) *Out of Sight, Out of Mind?*, Edinburgh: Scottish Transgender Alliance.

Roche, B. (2005) *Sexuality and Homelessness*, London: Crisis. Available at: http://www.opendoors.net.au/wp-content/uploads/2009/10/sexuality-homelessness-crisis-paper.pdf (accessed 29 July 2010).

Rosario, M., Schrimshaw, E.W. and Hunter, J. (2004a) 'Ethnic/racial differences in the coming-out process of lesbian, gay, and bisexual youths: a comparison of sexual identity development over time', *Cultural Diversity and Ethnic Minority Psychology*, 10, 215–28.

Rosario, M., Schrimshaw, E. W. and Hunter, J. (2004b) 'Predictors of substance use over time among gay, lesbian, and bisexual youths: an examination of three hypotheses', *Addictive Behaviors*, 29, 1623–31.

Rutter, P.A. and Soucar, E. (2002) 'Youth suicide risk and sexual orientation', *Adolescence*, 37, 289–99.

Ryan, S.D., Pearlmutter, S. and Groza, V. (2004) 'Coming out of the closet: opening agencies to gay and lesbian adoptive parents', *Social Work*, 49, 85–95.

Saewyc, E.M., Homma, Y., Skay, C.L., Bearinger, L.H., Resnick, M.D. and Reis, E. (2009) 'Protective factors in the lives of bisexual adolescents in North America', *American Journal of Public Health*, 99, 110–17.

SAGE (Services and Advocacy for Gay, Lesbian, Bisexual and Transgender Elders) (2010) *Improving the Lives of LGBT Older Adults*, New York: SAGE.

Schonfield, S. (2008) *Survey of Patient Satisfaction with Transgender Services*. London: NHS Audit Information and Analysis Unit.

Schope, R. (2005) 'Who's afraid of growing old? Gay and lesbian perceptions of aging', *Journal of Gerontological Social Work*, 45, 23–39.

SCIE (Social Care Institute for Excellence) (2003) *Human Rights: Changing the Ethos of Social Care*, London: SCIE.

Scottish Government (2002) 'Choose life: a national strategy and action plan to prevent suicide'. Available at: http://www.scotland.gov.uk/Resource/Doc/46932/0013932.pdf (accessed 13 July 2010).

Scottish Government (2009) *Personalisation: A Shared Understanding*. Edinburgh: Changing Lives Service Development Group.

Scourfield, J., Roen, K. and McDermott, E. (2008) 'Lesbian, gay, bisexual and transgender young people's experiences of distress: resilience, ambivalence and self-destructive behaviour', *Health and Social Care in the Community*, 16, 329–36.

Shakespeare, T. (2002) 'The social model of disability: an outdated ideology?', *Research in Social Science and Disability*, 2, 9–28.

Shakespeare, T., Gillespie-Sells, K. and Davies, D. (1996) *The Sexual Politics of Disability: Untold Desires*, London: Cassell.

Sherriff, N. and Pope, R. (2008) 'The lesbian, gay, bisexual, trans, and unsure (LGBTU) youth research project: views and experiences of young people living in West Sussex', *Education and Health*, 26, 63–6.

Sinecka, J. (2008) '"I am bodied". "I am sexual". "I am human". Experiencing deafness and gayness: a story of a young man', *Disability and Society*, 23, 475–84.

Smith, A. and Calvert, P. (2001) *Opening Doors*, London: Age Concern.

Smith, B. (1993) 'Homophobia: why bring it up?', in H. Abelove, M.A. Barale and D.M. Halperin (eds) *The Lesbian and Gay Studies Reader*, pp 99–102, New York: Routledge.

Social Work Reform Board (2010) 'Building a safe and confident future: one year on'. Available at: http://www.education.gov.uk/swrb (accessed 27 February 2011).

SSWIA (Scottish Social Work Inspection Agency) (2006) *Extraordinary Lives: Creating a Positive Future for Looked after Children in Scotland*, Edinburgh: Scottish Social Work Inspection Agency.

STA (Scottish Transgender Alliance) (2008) *Transgender Experiences in Scotland*. Edinburgh: Equality Network.

Stein, G.L., Beckerman, N.L. and Sherman, P.A. (2010) 'Lesbian and gay elders and long-term care: identifying the unique psychosocial perspectives and challenges', *Journal of Gerontological Social Work*, 53(55), 421–35.

Stonewall (no date) *Supporting Young Lesbian, Gay and Bisexual Young People*. London: Stonewall.

Stonewall Cymru (2009) *Double Stigma: The Needs and Experiences of Lesbian, Gay, and Bisexual People with Mental Health Issues Living in Wales*. Cardiff: Stonewall Cymru.

Stonewall Scotland (2005) *Housing and Support Needs of Older Lesbian, Gay, Bisexual and Transgender (LGBT) People in Scotland*. Edinburgh: Communities Scotland.

Stonewall and Triangle Wales (2006) *Meeting the Housing Needs of LGB People*, Cardiff: Stonewall Cymru.

Sutcliffe, L. (1995) *There Must Be Fifty Ways to Tell Your Mother: Coming out Stories*. London: Cassell.

Sutherland, M. (2009) *In Residence: Practice Applications for Residential Childcare*. Edinburgh: Scottish Institute for Residential Childcare.

Swigonski, M. (1995) 'The social service needs lesbians of color', in H. Hildalgo (ed) *Lesbians of Color: Social and Human Services,*. New York: The Haworth Press, pp 67–83.

Thompson, N. (1993) *Anti-Discriminatory Practice*. Basingstoke: Palgrave.

TOPSS (Training Organisation for Personal Social Services) (2002) *National Occupational Standards for Social Work*. Leeds: Skills for Care.

Trotter, J. and Gilchrist, J. (1996) 'Measuring outcomes in practice learning and assessment of lesbian and gay issues in social work training', *Social Work Education*, 15, 75–82.

Turner, L., Whittle, S. and Combs, R. (2009) 'Transphobic hate crime in the European Union', ILGA-Europe and Press for Change. Available at: http://www.ucu.org.uk/media/pdf/r/6/transphobic_hate_crime_in_eu.pdf (accessed 12 December 2011).

UKLGIG (UK Lesbian and Gay Immigration Group) (2009) *Annual Report*. London: UKGLIG.

UKLGIG (2010) *Failing the Grade: Home Office Initial Decisions on Lesbian and Gay Claims for Asylum*. London: UK Lesbian and Gay Immigration Group.

UNHCR (UN High Commissioner for Refugees) (2008) 'Guidance note on refugee claims relating to sexual orientation and gender identity'. Available at: http://www.unhcr.org/refworld/docid/48abd5660.html (accessed 3 December 2010).

Valios, N. (2001) 'Desire Denied', *Community Care*, 20 September, 6.

Van Den Bergh, N. and Crisp, C. (2004) 'Defining culturally competent practice with sexual minorities: implications for social work education and practice', *Journal of Social Work Education*, 40, 221–38.

Waites, M. (2003) 'Equality at last? Homosexuality, heterosexuality and the age of consent in the United Kingdom', *Sociology*, 37, 637–55.

Walters, K.L. and Person, R. (2008) 'Negotiating conflicts in allegiances among lesbians and gays of color: reconciling divided selves and communities', in G.P. Mallon (ed) *Foundations of Social Work Practice with Lesbian and Gay Person*, New York: Harrington Park Press, pp 41–68.

Warner, J., McKeown, E., Griffin, M., Johnson, K., Ramsay, A. and Cort, C. (2004) 'Rates and predictors of mental illness in gay men, lesbians and bisexual men and women: results from a survey based in England and Wales', *British Journal of Psychiatry*, 185, 479–85.

Weaver, H.N. and Burns, B.J. (2001) 'I shout with fear at night: understanding the traumatic experiences of refugees and asylum seekers', *Journal of Social Work*, 1, 147–64.

Welch, S., Howden-Chapman, P. and Collings, S.C.D. (1998) 'Survey of drug and alcohol use by lesbian women in New Zealand', *Addictive Behaviors*, 23, 543–8.

Welsh Assembly (2009) 'Talk to me: a national plan to reduce suicide and self harm in Wales (2008–2013)'. Available at: http://wales.gov.uk/consultations/healthsocialcare/talktome/?lang=en (accessed 13 July 2010).

Wexler, L.M., DiFluvio, G. and Burke, T.K. (2009) 'Resilience and marginalized youth: making a case for personal and collective meaning-making as part of resilience research in public health', *Social Science and Medicine*, 69, 565–70.

Wheeler, D.P. (2003) 'Methodological issues in conducting community-based health and social services research among urban black and African American LGBT populations', *Journal of Gay and Lesbian Social Services*, 15, 65–78.

Whittle, S., Turner, L. and Al-Alami, A. (2007) 'Engendered penalties: transgender and transsexual people's experiences of inequality and discrimination', Report commissioned by the Equalities Review. Available at: http://www.nmhdu.org.uk/silo/files/the-equalities-review.pdf (accessed 12 December 2011).

Whittle, S., Turner, L., Combs, R. and Rhodes, S. (2008) 'Transgender Eurostudy: legal survey and focus on the transgender experience of health care in EU', International Lesbian and Gay Organisation. Available at: http://www.scie-socialcareonline.org.uk/profile.asp?guid=d5792b53-0716-4682-8dd8-8cf0e9e34c54 (accessed 12 December 2011).

Williams, J. (2001) '1998 Human Rights Act: social work's new benchmark', British Journal of Social Work, 31, 831–44.

Williams, T.J., Pepitone, M.E., Christensen, S.E., Cooke, B.M., Huberman, A., Breedlove, N.J., Breedlove, T.J., Jordan, C. and Breedlove, S.M. (2000) 'Finger-length ratios and sexual orientation', Nature, 404, 455–6.

Williamson, I. (1999) 'Why are gay men a high risk group for eating disturbance?', European Eating Disorders Review, 7, 1–4.

Willis, P., Ward, N. and Fish, J. (2011) 'Searching for LGBT carers: mapping a research agenda in social work and social care', British Journal of Social Work, 41, 1304–20.

Wise, S. (2001) 'Heterosexism', in M. Davies (ed) The Blackwell Encyclopaedia of Social Work, Oxford: Blackwell, p 154.

Xavier, J., Honnold, J. A. and Bradford, J. (2007) 'The health and health-related needs and lifecourse experiences of transgender Virginians'. Available at: http://www.vdh.state.va.us/epidemiology/diseaseprevention/documents/pdf/thisfinalreportvol1.pdf (accessed 12 April 2010).

Ziyadeh, N.J., Prokop, L.A., Fisher, L.B., Rosario, M., Field, A.E., Camargo, J., Carlos A. and Bryn Austin, S. (2007) 'Sexual orientation, gender, and alcohol use in a cohort study of US adolescent girls and boys', Drug and Alcohol Dependence, 16, 119–30.

Index

Note: The following abbreviations have been used: f = figure; t = table